THE
STORYSELLING
METHOD

*Master the art of storytelling
to build trust, stand out,
and boost sales*

Philipp Humm

www.power-of-storytelling.com

TABLE OF CONTENTS

PRAISE FOR THE BOOK

"This book is an absolute gem that will elevate your sales game and entrepreneurial success. With its easy-to-follow structure, relatable examples, and practical tips, this book will help you harness the power of storytelling to connect with customers and close more deals."

– Leon Mishkis, Chief Operating Officer (COO), NewtonX

"The StorySelling Method is a must-read for any sales professional. It captures the essence of storytelling, showing you how to use stories to improve your relationships and set yourself apart from the competition. If you apply the learnings, it's guaranteed to affect your sales success."

– Gina Telford, Sales Director, Novartis

"Starting meetings with a powerful story is a great way to build strong relationships. The StorySelling Method is an excellent resource for mastering the art of storytelling in both business and life. An easy step-by-step guide, full of practical examples and tips. A book every manager should read and get their team to read!"

– Lucie Maillet St-Pierre, VP Customer Success, Salesforce

"Tired of the same old sales pitches? Get ready for a fresh approach to sales storytelling! This book is packed with practical tips, real-life examples, and powerful exercises to craft stories that sell."

– Lee B. Salz, Author of Sell Different!

To my sister Chantal, for always having my back; to my friend Damian, for inspiring me to be a better person; and to meditation, for helping me overcome the perceived limitations of my mind.

INTRODUCTION

"Inside each of us is a natural-born storyteller, waiting to be released."

– Robin Moore,
author of *The Green Berets*

December 2021.

I was sitting in my office in Amsterdam when I got a call from an unknown number. Normally, I ignore these calls, but for some reason, I answered this one.

"Hello?"

"Hi Philipp," a voice on the other end said, "This is Laura. I was in your StorySelling program a few months ago. I'm sorry to disturb you, but I was just so excited."

She went on, "You won't believe what just happened! My manager came up to me and asked if I was bribing our clients."

Not really sure what to say, I replied, "Ahh... I hope you didn't come here for legal advice?"

"No, no! Don't worry. I'm obviously not bribing anyone. My boss just didn't get it. Last year, I had one of the worst closing rates on the entire floor. I actually thought I'd lose my job. This year, I exceeded my quota by 73%. My boss even put me up for promotion."

"That's awesome, Laura! I'm curious… what changed?"

"Well, after the program, I made the commitment to use one tiny story in every sales meeting. Nothing crazy. But it worked incredibly well. I can literally see my client's guard dropping the moment I share a story. I kind of knew that stories were powerful… but not to that extent. So thanks, Philipp."

These are the moments that I live for. These are the moments that get me out of bed every single day.

Laura is just one of hundreds of people who I've seen unlock massive results through storytelling.

And **you** can do the same.

By the end of this book, you'll know how to use stories to:

- Leave magical first impressions
- Become your clients' #1 trusted advisor
- Communicate the value you're bringing to the table
- Overcome any sales resistance
- Inspire, motivate, and positively influence anyone around you

In *The StorySelling Method*, you'll discover the techniques I've used in my programs with leading organizations such as Google, Visa, E.ON, Oracle, ECCO, Noom, and Bain & Company. To develop these techniques, I interviewed 71 sales leaders and frontline sellers on how they use stories, what types of stories they tell, and what makes a good sales story. I've been fortunate to speak to sales experts including Mike Weinberg, author of *New Sales. Simplified.*, Anthony Iannarino, author of *Elite Sales Strategies*, and Branden Coté, VP of Sales and Product at Aston Martin.

The techniques you're about to learn have changed my life and my work, and they have turned literally thousands of my clients into charismatic StorySellers. Do you want to become a StorySeller and change your life?

The StorySelling Method

My signature system, the *StorySelling Method*, helps you move from beginner to expert storyteller. It focuses on five core areas to transform your storytelling skills:

1. **Craft stories**: Learn how to turn any moment (even the most boring one) into a captivating story.

2. **Find stories**: Develop the five types of stories that are most effective in sales conversations.

3. **Build confidence**: Understand how to confidently share stories in any conversation.

4. **Deliver stories**: Know how to weave the right stories into your conversations naturally and authentically.

5. **Take action**: Make a clear plan to transform your storytelling skills.

I suggest that you read this book from start to finish and do the exercises at the end of each chapter. However, if you're familiar with a certain topic, feel free to skip ahead.

This book focuses on *oral* storytelling, which means face-to-face, virtual, or over the phone. Even though the storytelling principles are similar for written stories, we won't be focusing on written storytelling. Why? I've never seen anyone close a deal or transform a buyer relationship by sharing a story via an email or a report. In sales, stories are the most effective when delivered verbally.

This book is for anyone who'd like to become more effective at selling a product, service, or idea. This includes:

- Sales and post-sales professionals
- Entrepreneurs
- Consultants
- Anyone seeking support from internal customers

Even if you don't directly work in sales, we all have to sell ourselves or our ideas in some way or another as part of our jobs. For example, we might need to get approval from another department, ask a colleague for data, or motivate our team. Storytelling is a powerful tool to pitch your ideas more effectively to gain buy-in. Your buyer may not be an external customer that buys your offering, but rather an internal customer that invests time and resources to collaborate with you.

When you master the art of storytelling, you will be able to build more trusting relationships, stand out, and boost sales.

It's a wonderful skill to have.

Storytelling is a skill that anyone can learn.

Having coached thousands of people, I can say with certainty that *everybody* has the potential to become great at storytelling. *You* have the ability to tell amazing stories. With the right techniques, a growth mindset, and practice, you'll become a phenomenal storyteller.

Ready? Let's go!

PART 1

CRAFT STORIES

Beginner storytellers believe that their stories have to be about extreme experiences to be considered interesting. For instance, how they climbed Mount Everest, ran five Ironmen, or built a multi-million-dollar company.

Expert storytellers don't limit themselves to these types of stories. Instead, they can take any experience, even the seemingly most insignificant one, and turn it into a compelling story. For instance, they could turn the moment they spilled coffee over their shirt into a truly inspiring story.

In Part 1, you'll build the skills to turn any moment into a captivating story. You'll learn how to structure, enhance, and simplify your stories. By the end of this section, you'll have one polished story that you can start using immediately.

Chapter 1

WHAT IS STORYTELLING?

"Storytelling is the most powerful way to put ideas into the world."

– Robert McKee,
author, screenwriter, and professor

If you've ever worked in a customer-facing job, you've probably heard some iteration of these phrases: "You've gotta tell more stories to connect with your customer," or "You need to tell your company's story to stand out."

I'm the first to admit that storytelling is a buzzword. So, let's start by clarifying what a story isn't and what it is.

A story is *not* a...

- **Case study:** Case studies are often ultra-impersonal, rather boring accounts of how your company helped another company. Ask yourself: how many case studies have you read in your life and how many do you remember? Not that many, right? Why do you not remember them? Because they're not personal enough. Humans care about humans, not about companies.

- **Testimonial:** Testimonials are short, bite-sized reviews of a customer's experience working with you. For instance, "I loved working with Philipp. He's got a German accent that's hotter than a pretzel straight out of the oven." I love testimonials, and they are a great way to give social proof, but they are just snippets of a story.

- **Product pitch:** Product pitches are presentations that go into great length to explain the features and why you're the *coolest company* to partner with. Just because your pitch follows a structure doesn't mean it's a story.

So, what is a story?

In its simplest form, a story is something interesting that happens to a specific person (not a company).

It's a narrative, or a series of events, that are connected and told in a particular order to entertain, inform, or inspire others.

More specifically in sales, stories are used to influence a sales event by highlighting the benefits of working with a product, service, or company.

Let's look at a sample sales story to make it clear.

This example comes from Luke Floyd, Senior Account Executive at Deel, a payroll solution provider. He has used this story with his buyers (accounting managers) to show how Deel's technology can help them save time.

In April 2021, I got on a call with an accounting manager for a US-based online study platform.

A few minutes in, she said, "I'm gonna be bold. I'm literally pulling out my hair right now."

I asked, "Why? What's going on?"

She said, "Do you know how painful it is to pay and manage 400 contractors via PayPal and Wise, like manually sending funds?"

She explained that it took her a full week every month to sort the payments out. On top of that, they were going through a huge acquisition that would increase the number of contractors from 400 to 900 *overnight*.

The same day, we sat down to work on a plan to sort this out—mostly to prevent any further hair loss. Within 10 days, we onboarded the 400 existing contractors on our payroll platform. By not having to deal with the admin of these contractors, the company had time to onboard the 500 new employees, and got the acquisition done.

The accounting manager called me a few weeks later and said, "Luke, before, it took me a week to get through the contractor payroll. Now, it takes me less than an hour. It's been game-changing. Thank you!"

Now you've got a feeling for what a sales story is, let's look at why it matters.

What is so important about storytelling that means successful sellers have made it a priority?

Why does storytelling matter in sales?

1. Storytelling makes your buyer remember you

Chip Heath,[1] co-author of *Made to Stick*, conducted an experiment at Stanford University to demonstrate the impact of storytelling on memory and persuasion. He asked some of his students to deliver to their classmates a 1-minute speech on the issue of non-violent crime in the US. He then asked the listeners to rate the speakers based on their delivery and persuasiveness.

After the exercise, Heath distracted the listeners for a few minutes with a random video, then abruptly asked them to write down every single idea from each speaker they had listened to.

When asked to remember the ideas, the listeners were shocked to find out how little they remembered about the speeches they'd listened to only a few minutes before.

Only 5% of them recalled any numbers or statistics. And that was in a class full of some of the smartest people on the planet.

On the other hand, 63% of the class remembered a story they had heard during the speeches.

Often, when we talk about our company, we say something like "We are the market leader for XYZ. We have 190 branches and sell our products to 22 different countries. We also invest 10% of our revenue in R&D [research and development]."

Well, that's great. These are important facts, and you should say them. But think: how memorable will that be for your customers? As Heath's experiment shows, people find it challenging to remember facts without a narrative.

If you want your potential buyer to remember you, tell them a story that touches them emotionally.

2. Storytelling increases the value of your offering

In July 2009, *New York Times* journalists Rob Walker and Josh Glenn ran an experiment.[2] They spent $129 on 100 ordinary objects from random thrift stores and garage sales. Their purchases included a bottle opener, a pink toy horse, a wooden mallet, a meat thermometer, a jar of marbles, and a Santa Claus nutcracker. Insignificant objects. Junk. Objects that all of us have in the deepest corners of our houses.

Then, they invited a group of volunteers to write short stories about each item. They listed the items for sale on eBay, but instead of including a plain, simple description of the product, they added the fictional stories.

The 100 items were originally purchased for $129 in total. How much do you think they sold for?

They sold for $3,613.

That's roughly a 2,700% increase in value, all from including a short fictional story.

This experiment illustrates that stories can increase the perceived value of any product or service.

3. Storytelling builds trust

In a series of experiments,[3] neuroeconomics pioneer Paul Zak explored the impact of stories on the brain. In an experiment, Zak and his team asked volunteers to watch one of two versions of a video about a dying boy. The first version had a clear narrative arc (aka a story), while the second had a "flat" narrative arc (i.e. no story). The team took blood samples from the volunteers before and after viewing the videos.

What do you think they found?

They found that those who watched the video with the story experienced an increase in oxytocin. Oxytocin is also known as the love hormone. When the brain synthesizes oxytocin, people become more trustworthy, generous, charitable, and compassionate.

When you tell a well-crafted story, your listener's brain releases oxytocin, making them more likely to trust you and your ideas.

Or as author and sales trainer Mark Hunter explains, "Stories put the other person in storytelling mode. It's no longer like, 'I gotta be careful. You're just trying to take my money.' By sharing a story you bring down any resistance and start having a conversation on the same level."

Now that you understand the importance of stories in sales, let's see how to structure any sales story.

Chapter 2

STRUCTURE STORIES

"In the first act you get your hero up a tree. The second act, you throw rocks at him. For the third act you let him down."

– George Abbott,
American theater producer and director

Depending on how experienced you are as a storyteller, you may have heard about different story structures or narrative arcs, as briefly mentioned in the previous chapter.

When I embarked on my storytelling journey, I started off with a 9-step story structure. But as I interviewed more sales executives, I realized that the most impactful stories cover just 4 essential steps: 1. Context, 2. Challenge, 3. Response, 4. Result.

In this chapter, you'll learn how to craft any sales story following the 4-step story structure.

Step 1: Context

In the first step, you want to give your listeners some rough context for the story. Describe when and where the events took place, who the main character was, and what they were up to.

The when, where, and who

Most of your stories can start with one sentence that clarifies when, where, and who.

For example:

- "Two years back, I got a call from the Head of Purchasing at one of the largest retailers in the UK."
- "Back in December 2016, right before Christmas, I was in the office in New York, doing some paperwork."
- "It was August 2022 when Spencer came back home to Minneapolis after a long trip across the country."

You can be more specific if you want to, but only if it serves a clear purpose. For instance, if your story is about how you get anxious in front of large groups, it could be helpful to provide context: "It was Monday at 6pm, during rush hour, and I was at Grand Central subway station, where the commuters were streaming past me."

The key is to keep it simple. This is StorySelling. Unless you're writing a novel, we don't need to know the color of your toothbrush holder.

Why does it matter to state the time, location, and main character? Because these three points give your story instant credibility. People will immediately believe that it's a true story. If you leave any of these points out, your listeners may spend more time questioning your story than listening to it.

The story becomes even more credible if you include the real name of the main character, their job role, and the company they work for (e.g., "Robin, who's the Head of Purchasing at Adidas"). However, before including anyone's real name, please check with the person whether they're happy for you to use their name.

The what

Next, tell us a little more about the main character and what is on their mind. What do they want in this specific situation, what are they afraid of, or what are they excited about?

For example:

- "I was a little surprised to have him on the phone, but then I thought 'This is great. I can now share the newest innovation from our R&D department. He'll be super impressed.'"

- "I was tired of life. It had been a very hectic year and I was ready for a break."

- "He felt good about the week. If he kept that performance up, he'd be promoted to partner in no time."

By sharing what's on the character's mind, your listeners will start caring. They'll become invested and want to know what is going to happen to the person next.

Two or three specific sentences are usually enough to achieve this.

There's one question that I get asked in every single workshop: "Does the story have to be about a person or can it be about a company?"

Well, you can talk about a company or product, but as Steve Clayton, VP at Microsoft, puts it, "To capture people's attention, you need to tell a story about people, not products." Your story will be much more impactful if you talk about a specific person, for example, a founder or Head of Product.

Step 2: Challenge

After you've given some quick context, it's time to introduce the challenge(s) that the main character is facing. It can be any type of challenge—a difficult decision, a problem in a relationship, or something physical—as long as it's substantial to the main character.

For example:

- "Then the Head of Purchasing said, 'Nora, we gotta terminate our contract with you. The quality of your footwear products doesn't meet our quality standards.' Immediately, my face turned red. 'That can't be right. He must be kidding me.'"

- "At that moment, I got an email from my manager with the 2023 target. My jaw dropped when I looked at the targets. What the hell? To get any bonus, I'd have to triple my sales. How could they share that information before Christmas?"

- "His daughter looked at him and said, 'Daddy, I don't want you to work on my birthday. I want you to be here with me.'"

When we start telling stories, we often think that these challenges have to be life-changing events like the time you almost died in a car accident. But telling these big stories is not necessary and can even be counterproductive in a sales context.

Why? Think about it: how many people do you know who've had a near-death experience? Not that many, right? So… it's not relatable.

Pick a challenge that is relatable—one that your listener has experienced or can imagine experiencing.

The challenge is the longest and most crucial part of the story. Describe the struggle, show what is at stake, and let the listener know how the character feels.

If the story is about yourself, introduce some degree of vulnerability. As Mark Manson, author of *The Subtle Art of Not Giving a F*ck* puts it, "Vulnerability is consciously choosing to *not* hide your emotions or desires from others."[10] It's about being open about your imperfections.

Your buyer is not looking for a cape-wearing superhuman to save the day. They're looking for someone qualified, but more so someone who they trust and relate to. Admitting you're not good at something or sharing mistakes you've made will immediately make you more trustworthy.

Step 3: Response

In the third step, let your listeners know how the main character responds to the challenge. What reactions do they have, and what actions or decisions do they take to overcome the challenge? Does anyone lend a hand?

For example:

- "Over the following 3 months, we worked with 12 engineers, 3 designers, and 2 marketers to design the new shoe. We shipped each prototype to roughly 250 customers to understand exactly what they liked about it and what could be improved..."

- "Each morning, I got up 30 minutes earlier than usual. I used those 30 minutes to research, classify, and contact leads. As a night owl, I hated everything about it, but it was worth it..."

- "To spend more time with his daughter, Spencer decided to cut non-essential travel by 50%. Before accepting any physical meeting request, he'd ask himself, 'Is my physical presence essential to the success of the meeting?'"

In real life, we usually try a bunch of things to resolve a challenge. In a story, if you share every one of them, it will become very long and complex. So, it's best to choose one or two crucial things that you or your subject does to turn the situation around. What are the *biggest* actions taken in response to the issue?

Why is it important to include the response?

Imagine interviewing someone for a role in your company. At the interview, they tell you, "When I started my current role, my team was in a very bad state. Morale was low, output wasn't satisfactory, and attrition was the highest in the entire company. Not anymore. I turned it around. Now, morale is 20% higher, output has increased by 30%, and attrition is in the lowest quartile of the company."

How would you feel about that? You'd feel cheated, right? Why? Because they didn't tell you what they did to resolve the issue—they only told you the result. Without knowing what they did to overcome the challenge, you might think that they got lucky.

Step 4: Result

In the last step, let your listeners know how the story turns out. Where do the actions in response to the challenge lead? What is the result?

For example:

- "A month ago, we launched the sale of our new shoe. In one month, we've made more sales than in the previous 5 months. People love the new shoe."

- "12 months later, my manager called and said, 'Mark, I've been extremely impressed with your results. So much so that I've decided to double your bonus for this year."

- "His daughter gave him a hug and whispered in his ear, 'Daddy, you're the best.'"

The result is your chance to show the transformation—to show how things changed throughout the story.

If the character felt overwhelmed in the middle of the story, they now feel in control.

If the character was sad, now they are happy.

If the character was as nervous as hell, now they're as cool as a cucumber.

Focus on one or two meaningful sentences that show the transformation. For most stories, that is enough, and it will reduce the impression of bragging or pushy selling.

The result doesn't always have to be a happy ending as long as the story serves a purpose. Every experience (good or bad) can teach us something. Share what you've learned from that experience. Otherwise, there's no point telling the story.

The last step is ideal to include any numbers or facts to give your story additional credibility. Your message lands stronger if you say, for instance, "With our help, the client managed to close 39% more deals" or "they reduced operating costs by 74%." By including numbers or facts, you provide evidence that you care about the actual business impact.

Bringing it together

Now that we've covered each step individually, let's look at the steps together:

Here's a sample story to show how the structure plays out in real life. The example comes from Colleen Stanley, author of *Emotional Intelligence for Sales Success*. She's used this story in her sales conversations to show her approach to improving companies' referral rates.

1. Context: In 2018, I was hired by a small pharma company in Los Angeles to run a referral training program for their sales teams. In one of my first meetings, I sat down with one of the account managers, Derek, to understand what was going on.

2. Challenge: In a not-very-empathetic way, I asked Derek, "Why are you not asking for referrals?"

Clearly embarrassed, he looked down, cleared his throat, and said, "Ahh, look. In my family, you don't ask for help. It's a sign of weakness."

3. Response: At that moment, I knew it wasn't the time to teach Derek any fancy referral tactics. Before anything, we needed to work on his belief system around asking for help. In my years of training and coaching, I learned that beliefs drive actions, both positive and negative. Over the next sessions, I collaborated with his team to first get them into the right mindset and then get them excited about asking for referrals.

4. Result: When it came to Derek, after a 2-hour session with me, he felt more comfortable. The same day, he sat down with his first client and asked for a referral. Guess what? He got it. In fact, that client gave him three qualified introductions, and one led to a $250k deal.

There are many different story structures. It's fine if you prefer another one, but make sure it's not too complex. My advice is to pick an easy structure and stick with it for a while until you're comfortable with it. The goal is to be so comfortable that you can use the structure anytime to improvise a story on the spot.

Exercise

Now it's time to start working on one of *your* stories.

Pick a challenge that you or a customer faced at work—ideally one that you've overcome. Don't overthink it. It doesn't have to be the "perfect" challenge. If your biggest challenge has been figuring out how to get a stubborn ketchup bottle open, that's OK. Use that challenge. At this point, I want you to get familiar with the story structure.

Got one?

Great. Go ahead and write down the story using the four steps of the story structure (context, challenge, response, and result). It should be enough to write down the main bullets of the story instead of writing down every single sentence, but I'll let you decide what works best for you. In the next chapter, you'll learn how to enhance that story.

Story structure template

Looking for prompts and guidance to help you craft your story? I've created a template to help you capture your stories using the four steps. Go to power-of-storytelling. com/kit and download the template.

⟨ Summary ⟩

◇ A simple but powerful structure for any sales story is the 4-step approach consisting of context, challenge, response, and result

◇ To have your story land, pick a character, challenge, or emotion that your listeners can relate to

◇ Practice the 4-step story structure until it becomes second nature before you work with other story structures

Chapter 3

ENHANCE STORIES

"A good story is one that takes you on an emotional rollercoaster. The decline is fast and terrifying, the twists are sharp and unexpected, and the end is happy and beautiful. If you have a story that does that to me, I don't care what you're selling. I'm going for another ride. I'm buying."

– Andrew Sykes,
Chief Executive Officer (CEO) of Habits at Work
and professor at Kellogg Sales Institute

Let's now move on to the fun stuff. In this chapter, you'll learn how to turn any moment (even the most mundane one) into an unforgettable story.

We'll first talk about the three elements that make a great story (surprise, emotions, and visual moments), then five specific techniques you can use to add these elements to your story.

Three elements of great storytelling

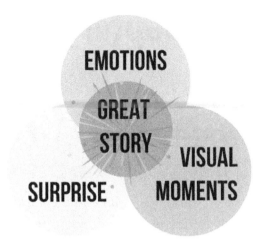

Element #1: Surprise

The moment you share a story or give a presentation, you're fighting for your listener's attention. Every second you're talking, they'll be tempted to check their smartphone, think about their next meeting, or daydream about their upcoming holiday.

How can you get people to hang on to every word you say?

... By bringing in elements of surprise.

Surprise refers to moments in the story that are unexpected. This can be anything that breaks the typical patterns of what your listeners expect.

Element #2: Emotions

Most people think of themselves as fairly rational. They think they're in control of their decisions and their decision-making is driven by logic. I've heard hundreds of times "I'm a numbers guy or gal" or "I'm very rational." Sure, that can be the case, but it's still not the numbers that make the decisions.

Harvard Business School professor Gerald Zaltman[4] found that 95% of purchasing decisions are subconscious. What's the biggest stimulus for subconscious decisions?

Emotions.

These purchasing decisions can be driven by pleasant emotions such as joy, pride, or excitement—or unpleasant emotions such as sadness, fear, or anger.

If you want to influence your buyer's purchasing decisions, your stories have to touch them emotionally.

Emotions help your listener connect with your story and make it more memorable.

Element #3: Visual moments

When we listen, read, or watch great stories, we don't just consume them on an intellectual level. We see the images in our head, feel the emotions, and actually experience the story as if it's happening to us. Our brain can't tell the difference between the reality we're experiencing live and the story we're listening to.

An effective story "transports" us into the character's world.

Let's say you tell your buyer a story about how you helped another customer overcome a problem. If you manage to make your buyer *see* the scene, they'll feel like it's happening to them. It becomes their reality. Without ever working with you, they feel connected and grateful to you for solving "their" problem.

Now you understand the elements that make a great story, let's look at five specific techniques you can use to include these elements in your stories.

Five techniques to enhance your story

Technique #1: Anticipation hook

One simple way to start your story with an element of surprise is to use an *anticipation hook*.

An anticipation hook is a sentence you say before your story to get your listeners excited about the story.

For example:

- "A couple of months ago, one of our customers found a very creative solution for exactly your problem..."
- "I learned a major lesson just a few months back..."
- "Working with that agency was mind-blowing..."

Note: I recommend using anticipation hooks sparingly. If you use them too often, you'll undermine your credibility because every story is framed as the "craziest" or "most interesting" experience.

Technique #2: Pattern interrupt

Another technique that adds surprise to your story is the *pattern interrupt*.

We humans have very clear ideas about what's normal. This includes how people should behave, what actions they should take, and what results they should expect. While you tell your story, your listeners will anticipate how the story is going to evolve.

You can add surprise to your story by breaking the typical patterns of what your listeners expect.

A pattern interrupt leads your listener in one direction (aka the setup), then it breaks that expectation (aka unusual activity).

For example:

Setup	Unusual activity
"My boss is the most chilled boss on earth. I thought he wanted to talk about soccer when he called me..."	"... but instead, he said, 'You, sir. You can pack your bags.'"
"My client told me to call five people..."	"... so just to be sure I got it right, I called 78."
"Every day, I go online to check our numbers. It's always a waste of my time as nothing has changed..."	"... but one day, I saw a massive drop on one of the graphs. Within one day, production volumes had declined by 75%."

The setup doesn't have to be right before the unusual activity. It can happen earlier in the story. For example, you may depict the character as peaceful and spiritual in context, then talk about something else, but then reveal their explosive outburst in the challenge.

No doubt, there are more techniques to add surprise. But keep in mind that you're telling a quick sales story, not writing a novel. For instance, "Something in that room didn't feel right. Moving quietly like a mouse, I put one foot in front of the other..." would be too much for a sales story.

What about humor? Humor comes alive from surprise moments. If you can include a few jokes in your story, that's awesome. Go for it. But keep in mind that your task as a storyteller is to tell a story that moves your listeners emotionally. Don't think that your story has to be hilarious. As Matthew Dicks, author of *Storyworthy*, puts it, "Humor is optional. Heart is non-negotiable."[11]

Technique #3: Inner dialogue

The third technique is a simple way to make your story more emotional: *inner dialogue.*

Inner dialogue refers to the thoughts the character has; in our case, in crucial moments of the story.

The average human has 6,200 thoughts a day.[5] A lot of these thoughts are anxious, obsessive, or impulsive. You can bring your listeners into the emotional moment by sharing some of these thoughts. What does your character fear, worry, dream, hope, or plan in key moments of the story?

For example:

- "I hope my boss reads this. He'll be so impressed."
- "That deal will change my life. The first thing I'll do with the money is buy my mum a new car."
- "Ah, I can't believe I did this. Everyone will think I'm a failure…"

By sharing what the character thinks, you make your listeners care. The more they know about the character, the more they'll be rooting for them.

After hearing the inner dialogue, your listeners will want to find out what happens.

While you should always be as truthful as possible, you have some creative freedom to make the inner dialogue more emotional. As presentation skills expert Patricia Fripp explains, "Stories need to be true, not 100% accurate." Feel free to exaggerate the thoughts to make it more dramatic.

Imagine you told a story about a mistake you made. Some genuine inner dialogue could have included, "Oh shoot; this is bad!" If you wanted to take it up a notch and make it more emotional, you could say, "Oh shoot. That sucks! No doubt he'll call my boss and complain about getting the worst service in his life. Goodbye bonus. Goodbye promotion."

A good rule of thumb when bending the truth is to ask yourself: if someone was with you when the actual event happened, would they recognize the story as truthful? If they'd look at you with a "WTF are you talking about?" expression, this would indicate that you've gone too far.

Technique #4: Outer dialogue

The fourth technique is my favorite way to make any story instantly more visual: *outer dialogue.*

Outer dialogue refers to the words or conversation between two or more characters; in our case, in key moments of the story.

While you could include a full-blown conversation between characters, it's often enough to have 1–3 sentences that reveal an important piece of information.

For example:

Without outer dialogue	*With* outer dialogue
"My boss told me that my pitch wasn't good enough."	"My boss said, 'Nora, you gotta work on your pitch. You won't close any deals if you stick to that pitch.'"
"In the end, we helped our client secure $3M in funding."	"My client called me and said, 'Mark, we just got the $3M in funding. It's crazy. Without you, we would've never gotten it!'"
"My coworker complimented me in front of the entire team."	"At that moment, my coworker stood up and said, 'I wanted to give a shout out to Nithya. She's the reason we've made it this far.'"

You see? It's a small modification, but it makes a massive difference to your story. By sharing the words that were used in the moment, you bring your story to life.

An ideal place to use outer dialogue is during the *challenge* (e.g., "My boss came up to me and said, 'Mario, what the hell? Your presentation was full of typos!'") or the *result* (e.g., "My client yelled down the phone, 'We did it. We've just been featured in *Time* magazine. I can't believe this is happening!'")

What if you can't remember the exact words that were used in specific situations? Similar to what we discussed with inner dialogue, you have some creative freedom here. Think what *could* have been said in the moment. What are the words that you, your boss, or your client could have used in this crucial moment? Try to use words that are sharp and trigger an emotional response.

Technique #5: Show emotions

The last technique helps to make the story more visual and emotional: show, don't tell.

When they want to share an emotion, most people *tell* listeners how the character felt. They use words like happy, sad, disappointed, nervous, etc.

While this is a great starting point as any emotion is better than no emotion, we can do better than that. Words like these aren't very visual. We can't picture what it looks like to be "disappointed" or "proud." It's kind of abstract.

Instead of telling the emotion, show the emotion. How does the body or face change when experiencing the emotion of the story?

Let's look at a few comparisons between *tell* and *show*.

Tell the emotion	*Show* the emotion
"My boss was extremely pleased."	"My boss came up to me and patted me on my back with a big smile on his face."
"Robin was very surprised with the results."	"Robin stood there with eyebrows raised and mouth wide open."
"Right before the presentation, I got very nervous."	"I started trembling and my entire face turned red."

It's a small tweak that makes the story instantly more visual.

To help you find the right words, here are the physical reactions to some of the most common emotions:

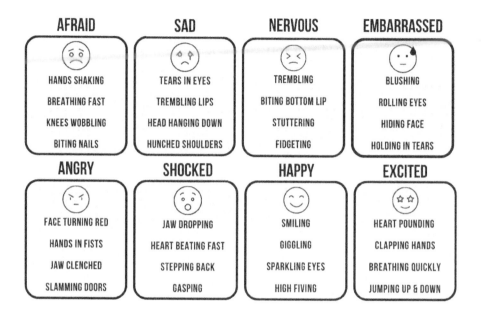

Looking for more words to show the emotions?

Just ask yourself: how do I react physically when I experience a certain emotion? What happens to my body or face when I'm sad, happy, etc.? Or, alternatively, think how one of your friends or family members physically reacts when experiencing a certain emotion. For example, when some people get angry, they yell whereas others become silent and clench their teeth.

You might be thinking, "I don't dare tell an emotional story to a business audience." Many people feel that way, and I carried that thought for a few years as well. But after trying out different formats, I realized that people at work are just the same as everywhere else. They want to feel a connection, laugh, and be inspired. They appreciate you bringing some emotion and excitement into their average days.

But what if you have a super-left-brain crowd (e.g., scientists or engineers)? In this case, go a little less deep into the emotions. Instead of talking for a full minute about how badly the challenge affected you emotionally, use one or two emotional sentences. Give them more insights into the actual problem, numbers, and actions.

On the contrary, if you have a super-right-brain audience (e.g., marketeers or sellers), you can go deeper into your emotions.

Bringing it together

Now that we've covered the three most important elements (surprise, emotions, and visual moments) and specific techniques to enhance your story, let's see how they play out in real life.

This example comes from Niraj Kapur, LinkedIn coach and author of *Everybody Works in Sales*. He uses this story occasionally to show his clients what really matters in sales. When you read it, try to spot how Niraj brings in different techniques to enhance his story. After the story, we'll recap some of his techniques.

Four years ago, a friend called and told me that Karren Brady was giving a talk. If you don't know her, Karren Brady is a major celebrity here in the UK. She's a co-host on the TV show *The Apprentice*.

So, I went to see her speech that night.

45

Very eloquently, she spoke for 15–20 minutes. After that, she said, "Does anybody have any questions?"

Complete silence.

After what felt like an eternity, I cautiously raised my hand and said, "Karren, I have a question... I wanted to spend more time with my family. I wanted less stress in my life.

... So, I set up my own business."

Immediately, the entire room burst out laughing.

I went on, "I've had this great career. I've got a bestselling book. But I have no business. I have no leads. I don't know what I'm doing wrong. What advice do you have for people like me struggling to set up their businesses?"

She replied, "I love that question. Asking questions is so important."

Then she gave me her answer.

At the end of her talk, she came over to me and said, "I really like the question you asked. Actually, we're looking for a sales trainer at my company. Do you have a business card?"

I was thinking, "Really? Of course, I have a business card for Karren Brady."

And I gave her my business card.

To which she said, "Thanks. I'll be in touch with you next week."

Well...

It's been **four and a half years now**.

Karren still *hasn't* called me.

I'm sure someone stole her phone. Or maybe she's out of data. Or maybe she feels too embarrassed to ask someone for help.

But jokes aside, what I learned from that experience is to ask great questions. When you ask great questions, you're going to help the people around you and you're earning respect in the room.

Did you notice which techniques Niraj used?

For instance:

- **Surprise**: A few unexpected twists (e.g., "I wanted to spend more time with my family. I wanted less stress in my life... So, I set up my own business.")

- **Emotions**: Some inner dialogue (e.g., "I'm sure someone stole her phone. Or maybe she's out of data. Or maybe she feels too embarrassed to ask someone for help.")

- **Visual moments**: Lots of outer dialogue (e.g., "I really like the question you asked. Actually, we're looking for a sales trainer at my company. Do you have a business card?")

But don't worry about including all of the techniques in each of your stories. Often, using only one or two of the techniques is enough. For instance, I've seen some very average stories land incredibly well only because of the surprise elements.

As you read the rest of the stories in this book, ask yourself: what techniques is the storyteller using to enhance the story? This way, you train your mind to think in these elements.

Exercise

Take the story you structured in the exercise in chapter 2 and think about how you can enhance it. See whether there are any moments where you can bring in:

1. Surprise (e.g., unusual activity)
2. Emotions (e.g., inner dialogue)
3. Visual moments (e.g., outer dialogue)

Summary

◈ You can tell any story in an engaging way by including the elements of surprise, emotions, and visual moments.

◈ Specific techniques to spice up your story include:

- Anticipation hook (a short hook to anticipate the story)
- Pattern interrupt (an unexpected event or activity)
- Inner dialogue (the character's thoughts)
- Outer dialogue (the specific words that were used)
- Show emotions (how the emotion physically looks)

Chapter 4

SIMPLIFY STORIES

"Tell me that story in half the number of words… now do it again… now do it again."

– Evan Kelsay,
Senior Director of Global Accounts at Seismic Software

While the stories I hear in each workshop and coaching session are very different, there's one thing that 99% of the stories have in common…

They tend to be too complex.

They go into too many unnecessary details or use language that is difficult to understand. Well, that's 99% of the stories. Obviously not your stories. But just for the unlikely scenario that this is a problem, here are a few techniques to simplify your stories.

Length

After analyzing the most impactful sales stories from my interviews, I found that the average story is 1 minute and 27 seconds. Rarely did anyone tell an impactful story that was longer than 3 minutes.

Sure, if your story is mind-blowing and your buyer adores you, you can take a little longer to share your story. If that's not the case, keep your stories between 1 and 2 minutes.

By going on for much longer, you risk losing your buyer's attention.

So, how can you shorten your story and eliminate any unnecessary details (aka "killing your darlings")?

Here are three ways you can eliminate unnecessary details:

1. Give less context

A lot of people give way too much context. They get lost in the details of how the product works, what their company does, or what responsibilities they have. I've seen cases where people have spent 5 minutes giving context. When you give too much context, your listeners will likely think, "What's going on here? What's the point of all this? Why do I need to know this?"

You're telling a business story. Eliminate any context that isn't helping the buyer understand or sympathize with the main character. You can do this by starting your story as close to the challenge as possible, without a long preamble.

Ask yourself: is this context needed for the story to make sense? If not, cut it.

2. Eliminate side characters

Often, our stories involve additional people, such as your boss, a friend, or the taxi driver. Unless these characters have a crucial role in the story, cut them out. I know... it's harsh, and you want to be inclusive. But any extra character brings in additional friction and makes it tougher for the audience to follow. You don't want anyone to think, "Wait. Who's Mary now?"

Ask yourself: is this character essential to the story? If not, cut them.

3. Focus on crucial moments

Life is complex. We often have more than one problem and we often try a million things to overcome these problems.

For instance, when I was in my 20s, I struggled with low levels of confidence. I tried a lot of different techniques to become more confident (therapy, visualization, affirmations, etc.). I have dozens of moments that I could include. But when I tell a story about my journey to become more confident, I focus on 1–3 crucial moments to keep it simple.

Ask yourself: what are the 1–3 most crucial moments in the story? Eliminate any moments that are not essential.

Language

After analyzing the length of the great sales stories, I also wanted to understand the language used in these stories. Plugging each story from my interviews into software that assesses readability,[6] I got some pretty interesting results:

The average sales story can be understood by a 5th grader (age 11 to 12).

The building blocks for the grade level are word length and sentence length. The shorter the word length and sentence length, the easier it is to understand. The easier it is to understand, the more you'll connect with your listener.

Here are two things you can do to make your story easy to understand:

1. Break down long sentences

One way to simplify a story is to break long sentences down into shorter sentences. Aim for sentences that are up to 15 words long, and avoid run-on sentences.

For example:

Long sentences	Shorter sentences
"When I took the leap and started my sales and coaching business four years ago, the beginning was tough because being a good salesperson and being a good business owner are two completely different things."	"Four years ago, I took the leap and started my own sales coaching business. But the beginning was tough. Being a good salesperson and being a good business owner are two completely different things."
"I knew it wasn't the time to teach Derek any fancy referral tactics because before anything, we needed to work on his belief system around asking for help."	"I knew it wasn't the time to teach Derek any fancy referral tactics. Before anything, we needed to work on his belief system around asking for help."

Ask yourself: can I break up any long sentences into shorter ones?

2. Use everyday language

If you say something like "I was responsible for optimizing mission-critical manufacturing processes," you're killing any story. Even if you're dealing with a technical topic, it's important to sound as natural as possible. Try to avoid technical terms, foreign words, or business jargon as much as possible.

For example:

Business language	Everyday language
"20% of the workforce was impacted by the company-wide layoffs."	"20% of the employees lost their jobs."
"I was worried that this could have a negative impact on my career."	"I thought, 'F*ck, I'll lose my job because of this.'"
"He was adamant not to leverage our new product."	"He said, 'Under no circumstances will I display your products on my shelves.'"

Ask yourself: can I replace any technical terms or business jargon with simpler words?

Exercise

Take the story you enhanced in the previous chapter and think about how you can simplify it. Consider whether there any moments where you can:

1. Cut unnecessary details (e.g., give less context, eliminate side characters)

2. Simplify your language (e.g., break up long sentences, use everyday language)

Summary

◇ Effective sales stories tend to be shorter, usually between 1 and 2 minutes long

◇ To simplify your story, cut any unnecessary details and use language that a 5th grader would understand

PART 2

FIND STORIES

Beginner storytellers may not know what stories to tell. When they share stories, they often share party or holiday stories. Not that there's anything wrong with this. I'd love to listen to drunk stories from your time in college, but at the end of the day, these stories don't really inspire action and may not be too relevant in your sales conversations.

Expert storytellers have a range of stories they can use in key moments of the sales conversation.

Knowing that you most likely don't have time to prepare hundreds of stories, I've boiled it down to the five story types that will get you the biggest results.

In Part 2, you'll learn how to develop the five most fundamental sales stories: connection stories, success stories, differentiation stories, industry stories, and resistance stories.

THE 5 CRUCIAL SALES STORIES

Chapter 5

CONNECTION STORIES

"Communication is merely an exchange of information, but connection is an exchange of our humanity."

– Sean Stephenson,
author of *Get Off Your "But"*

I'd like you to think about the last meeting you had with a buyer. How did you spend the first few minutes of the meeting? What did you talk about?

There's a high chance that the conversation went something like this:

You: "Hi, how are you?"

Buyer: "Good. How are you?"

You: "Great, thanks."

If you felt particularly talkative that day, you might have talked about the weather, the traffic, or the lunch you just had.

Talking about the weather is not bad, but it's standard. And with standard, you're not building rapport. Your relationship stays at the same level.

So, what can you do instead? How can you stand out and make your buyer trust you?

Share a short connection story at the beginning of the meeting.

Connection stories are short, personal accounts of recent experiences that reveal more about who you are.

Here are two sample connection stories.

Example 1:

Storyteller: Dorina Rigo, CEO and founder of Fit Boots

> **Dorina:** "Hi there. How's it going?"
>
> **Buyer:** "I'm good. How are you?"
>
> **Dorina:** "Awesome. I had a really cool thing happen this morning. I went to my favorite coffee place to order my daily muffin. And right when I got my card out, the owner, Joe, shook his head and said, 'Dorina, it's all good. This one is on the house.' I said, 'For real? Why?' And he said, 'Just because.' He made my day. I realized that you can change someone's day by a tiny gesture. Anyway, has that ever happened to you? Was someone very nice to you for no real reason?"
>
> **Buyer:** "Hmm… let me think. Actually, a few days back, this old lady…"

Example 2:

Storyteller: Max Kurth, sales manager at Amazon

Buyer: "Hi, how are you?"

Max: "Really good. Though yesterday sucked a bit. When I was young, I played lots of tennis, even at a competitive level. Yesterday, after years of not playing, I thought I'd get my racket out and hit a few balls. I've still got it, right? Man was I wrong. It was miserable. I hit every second ball into the net. Classic case of expectations versus reality. Anyway, enough about me... how about you? Do you have a hobby you love but you're not particularly good at?"

Buyer: "For me, it was soccer. A couple of months back, I went to the open day at my son's school..."

These two examples give you an idea of how to use stories to build a connection right at the start of the meeting. Both Dorina and Max use stories like this when someone asks them "How are you?" and have noticed drastic changes in how the meeting started.

Connection stories are great to set the right tone for the meeting and create an environment where the buyer feels safe to share something more personal as well.

How to find connection stories

You can use any experience that shows personality as your connection story. *Anything* that is more interesting than the weather or the traffic.

Here are some prompts to get you started. You can ask yourself:

- Has anything interesting happened lately?

- Have you recently picked up any new skills?

- Has some little thing annoyed you?

But don't limit yourself to these prompts. Every day, you probably have moments that stand out or touch your heart in some way.

How to deliver connection stories

Keep 'em short: This story type is super short, about 30 seconds, maybe 60 if it's an incredible story. But for real... keep it short. Sharing long stories before establishing a connection can be counterproductive.

Focus on asking great questions: After your story, ask them, "How about you? Have you ever been in [situation of your story]?" For the question to work, it's important to pick a question they can likely respond to with a story themselves. If you pick a question that is too niche, you won't get a story in return. For example, a less effective question would be "What about you? Have you driven a Ford Mustang?" Chances are that your buyer hasn't driven a Ford Mustang, and even if they have, they won't have a story about it. A better question would be "What about you? What has been your most amazing driving experience?" It's much more likely that your buyer can bring in their own story with this question.

As a heads-up, at the beginning, it may feel a little awkward to share these types of stories. Sharing something personal, vulnerable, and unsolicited is not something we do very often. But it's worth it to build rapport.

When I first heard about connection stories, my immediate reaction was "Wait? Talk about myself, unsolicited? Eff this. This is crazy." As an introvert, something like that had never crossed my mind.

But then my curiosity kicked in and I thought, "Well, I'll give it a try. What's the worst thing that could happen?"

To reduce the stakes, I started using connection stories with my friends. Every time I met a friend, I'd think "How could I respond to 'How are you today?'"

Sure, half the time, I forgot to share a story. But the times I remembered it, the conversations started off very differently. Instead of wasting time on blah-blah, we'd often move on to more meaningful topics much quicker.

Seeing my friends' positive responses, I decided to try this out with my coworkers. After just a few weeks of "testing" connection stories with my coworkers, I extended them to my customers.

By now, I've used this type of story in hundreds of sales conversations. The overall response has been very positive. Around 8 out of 10 customers have responded positively to the story. Most of the time, they respond with a story or interesting fact in return. Sure, maybe 2 out of 10 react more neutrally to these stories, but they don't react negatively to them. So, there is really no downside in my experience. If they don't engage with your story, just move on to the actual topic of the meeting.

I knew it was worth it when a client told me in summer 2022, "Philipp, I knew that I wanted to work with you in the first minute of talking to you. I'm not sure what you did but it felt like speaking to a very close friend."

Exercise

Think of a few experiences from the past week that stood out. Has anything interesting or unusual happened lately?

Got something? Awesome. Now, go ahead and write down your short story and a question that you could ask your imaginary listener (e.g., "How about you? Have you ever…?")

Free masterclass: The 3-step formula to build instant trust through storytelling

Do you want some extra help to build trusting relationships without awkwardly talking about the weather? I've got your back. Join me for a fun 30-minute live recording where I'll help you prepare powerful connection stories. Go to power-of-storytelling.com/kit and check out the masterclass for free!

Oh, and you'll get a sneak peek of the book's creator (aka me) and a taste of how cool (or intense) my workshops can be.

Summary

◇ Connection stories are short, personal accounts of recent experiences that reveal more about who you are

◇ The objective of connection stories is to build rapport with your buyers and make them feel comfortable opening up to you

◇ You have a great opportunity to share a short connection story when someone asks "How are you?"

Chapter 6

INDUSTRY STORIES

"You've got to provide actual value with your story. Help your client understand their environment, making sense out of the world."

– Anthony Iannarino,
author of *Elite Sales Strategies*

After exchanging some small talk, sellers usually try to find out what's going on with their buyers' business (aka *discovery*). What problems they are struggling with, what they have tried, what they would like to change, and so on.

This is great and every seller should do this. But sometimes, the discovery stage may overwhelm your buyers. They may get annoyed if you ask too many questions. They may not feel comfortable sharing their deepest pains. Or they may not even be aware of their problems. To bypass any of these hurdles, you can pause your questions for a moment and ease the discovery by sharing an *industry story*.

Industry stories delve into the challenges or trends that you've observed in your buyer's industry or business landscape.

By using industry stories, you position yourself as a trusted advisor to your client. Instead of being just another salesperson, you'll become your buyer's consultant.

Let's look at two examples.

Example 1:

Storyteller: Scott Von Deylen, VP of Business Development at Tabula Rasa Healthcare

Point: There are two pain points that his clients (independent pharmacies) are experiencing

> **Scott**: "So, I'm just the guy in the middle. But I talk to dozens of pharmacies on a weekly basis and they're telling me what their pain points are. Would it be helpful if I shared what is impacting these other pharmacies, similar to the one you own?"
>
> **Pharmacy owner**: "Sure. Go ahead."
>
> **Scott**: "Great. So first, a very common pain point for our customers is the shrinking reimbursements on their prescription medications. They used to get paid $10 for the average drug. Now they're getting paid $3. Why? Because pharmacies are getting penalized by Medicare's adherence measurements. If your patients who are 65 and older come in less than 80% of the time to fill their prescriptions, then you, the owner, gets a penalty. A penalty they take out of your bank. Is that a problem for you as well?"
>
> **Pharmacy owner**: "Yeah. For sure. Medicare has eaten up the little profit we made before."

Scott: "Yeah, that's affecting most independent pharmacies. The second pain point is not having the time and ability to offer clinical services such as testing for flu, expanded immunization programs, or diabetes management. Even though clinical services are a very attractive opportunity, most pharmacies struggle to offer them. They don't find the time to train the staff, offer the services, and put the right billing in place. Are any of these a pain point for you as well?"

Pharmacy owner: "Yes. We've struggled a lot with setting up a billing system. It takes hours every week just to get the billing right."

Example 2:

Storyteller: Chantal Humm (my beloved sister), former account executive at Google

Point: Many clients (advertisers) falsely assume that content needs to become shorter and shorter

Chantal: "Have you focused more on shorter or longer video content in your online marketing campaigns?"

Advertiser: "Mostly on shorter content to keep viewers engaged."

Chantal: "Got it. That's very common. We've seen lots of our clients designing shorter and shorter videos to capture people's attention. You've probably also heard a few times that 'Consumers have shorter attention spans than goldfish' or 'anything longer than 2 minutes won't be watched,' right? But is it true that only shorter videos get watched?

"We looked at the data and found that Hollywood movies and books are actually getting longer. A lot of us can easily binge-watch 10+ hours of *Game of Thrones* over a weekend. Our attention spans are not the problem. The problem is that the content is not engaging enough.

"Consumers don't care how long the content is, but how much it hooks them from the start. So instead of trying to create shorter content, we recommend creating content that introduces and (re)introduces hooks from the start. Rather than waiting for the climax midway through the video, give listeners dopamine hits throughout the video."

Note: While all other story types in this book are about specific people, these stories are about an entire industry or a larger sample of companies. They don't follow the typical narrative arc and don't zoom in to very visual moments, but industry stories are important to have in your client conversations.

How to find industry stories

Ask yourself:

- What's impacting my customer's current business environment?

- What technology changes are about to disrupt their business?

- How is customer behavior changing?

You probably have dozens of sales conversations per week. Every sales conversation is an opportunity to gather information about your buyer's industry. Every conversation is an additional data point that you can use to tell industry stories in your next conversations.

What if you're struggling to come up with insights about the buyer's industry? Then do additional research, read industry news, discuss any trends in your next team meeting, interview your coworker, visit industry conferences, review the latest deals in the market, and interview industry experts—the opportunities are endless. (More on that in chapter 10.)

How to deliver industry stories

Reference authority: If you can, try to reference some sort of authority in your story. As Larry Kendall, author of *Ninja Selling*, puts it, "100 economists have more authority than your opinion alone." Authority could come from business leaders, economists, or other well-known industry experts.

Focus on problems you can help solve: The goal is not to share any random challenges impacting the buyer just for the sake of making conversation. It's to share challenges that your product or service can help solve. Every story should be strategic and help you strengthen the relationship with the buyer and move closer to the sale.

Validate your observations: Check in with your buyer on how they've experienced the challenge or trend you outlined. If they confirm it and consider it important, it helps you frame and tailor your offering. If they don't consider it important, do some more digging to understand what *is* really impacting the client.

Exercise

1. Pick an important buyer group (industry or vertical)

2. Think about the 1–2 problems/trends/threats impacting that group

3. Write down what the "old world" looked like, what changed, and what the "new world" looks like

Find stories workbook

Would you like more guidance/prompts to help you develop the five fundamental sales stories? I've created a workbook that will help you develop plenty of story ideas. Go to power-of-storytelling.com/kit and download the workbook for free.

Summary

◇ Industry stories delve into the challenges or trends that you've observed in your buyer's industry or business landscape

◇ The goal of industry stories is to position yourself as your buyer's trusted advisor

◇ You can share an industry story early on when you have a rough understanding of your buyer's business and some of the problems they are experiencing

Chapter 7

SUCCESS STORIES

"When you say it, it's marketing. When your customer says it, it's social proof."

– Andy Crestodina,
Chief Marketing Officer (CMO) of Orbit Media

We're social animals. Every time we make a decision, we ask ourselves either consciously or subconsciously, "How would someone else decide in this situation?" This is why we check the reviews on Amazon before making a purchase or check out the Google rating before going to a restaurant. We're like, "Why would I listen to my own intuition when I can blindly follow the opinion of a random person on the internet?"

The same applies to any sales conversation. Your buyer is likely thinking "How would someone else (my boss, my co-worker, or a competitor) solve that problem? What would they do?"

That's when you bring in a *success story*.

Success stories are real-life examples of how a customer successfully used your product or service to solve a particular problem and achieve their desired outcomes.

The ideal time to share a success story is when you're crystal clear on one of your buyer's pain points.

Let's look at two examples.

Example 1:

Storyteller: Julia Winkler, former account manager at marketing agency Tricycle Europe

Point: We can help any company (even more traditional ones) become great at selling via social media

> "In August 2017, our agency was hired by one of the top three tech companies in Germany. We were asked to help the sales org improve their social selling. What that meant was to help them find and engage with target customers via social media.
>
> A week later, I met with the CMO in Munich. In his office, the CMO told me, 'Look, Julia. We're dinosaurs. 99 out of 100 people in my team would much rather pick up the phone and call someone than send a message on LinkedIn.'
>
> At that moment I asked him, 'How many times have you posted something on LinkedIn in the last month?'
>
> Cautiously, he responded, 'Well, I haven't posted anything this month...'
>
> After that I said, 'Look, I've analyzed the social media activity of your management team. It turns out that your team is 63% less active on social media than your competitors. If you want to drive change in your organization, your management needs to lead the change.'

The same day, we agreed to train the management team first on social selling and only then move on to the rest of the organization.

With management leading the way, the company managed to increase their social media activity drastically. In fact, two years later, the CMO called me and said, 'Julia, this is good stuff. Our social media activity has doubled since you came onboard. We're now making hundreds of millions through leads from social media.'

That's one example of how that client transformed their social selling. Do you feel that a similar approach could work for you?"

Example 2:

Storyteller: Victor Ruiz Lafita, Sales Lead at Bigblue

Point: By outsourcing your logistics to us, you'll have more time and mental space to grow your business

"In late 2021, I joined a call with the CEO of an athletic clothing retailer in Barcelona.

A short time into the call, she said 'Look, I'm the CEO here. Guess how I spent my morning today?'

Confused, I said 'Don't know. Defining the 2022 strategy, negotiating deals. You tell me.'

She said, 'I was in our warehouse for 4 hours, calling upset customers, packing boxes, and trying to make sense out of our logistics mess. Not very flashy, right?'

She told me a bit more about her current logistics setup. It turned out that they were running logistics themselves. But in doing it themselves, they had tons of problems. Items went missing, there were delays in delivery, and there was no transparency on the deliveries.

The same day, we agreed to partner with them and take over the entire logistics of her company. We started to run the warehouse and bring transparency into the deliveries. Before then, the end customers had no idea when a product would arrive. Through our technology, they knew exactly where the product was and when to expect it.

It's been over a year since we partnered. Customer satisfaction is at 95%, the error rate is below 0.01%, but most importantly, her team can now focus on what matters.

I actually talked to her in June and she said, 'We spent the entire day defining our marketing campaign. I know this doesn't sound special, but it is for us. We now have the time to focus on what matters'.

Do you feel that outsourcing logistics could be an option for you?"

How to find success stories

Take a look at your customer relationship management (CRM) system (or comparable), review the customers you've worked with, and identify the ones who were satisfied with your help.

Then, ask yourself:

- What situation were these customers in before meeting you?

- What problems did they have? How did they feel at the time?

- How did you help them overcome their problems?

- How were their lives transformed? How did they feel after?

You can also look at the case studies within your company and see whether you can adjust any of them to make them more personal.

How to deliver success stories

The customer is the hero: For those of us who've been raised as if we were the center of the universe, this might be a tough one: You're not the hero in the story. In most success stories, the customer is the hero, not you. You're the guide who helps the hero figure out what they need to do to be successful. So, share the story from the customer's perspective.

It's relevant: Before you share any success story, be crystal clear on the identity of the buyer you're trying to influence. What's their company size, industry, geography, and pain points? When you're clear on that, you can pick a story about a customer who has a similar profile. Sure, most of the time it's tough to find a story that fits your buyer perfectly but try to tick at least a few boxes. If you share something that isn't relevant to your buyer, it can work against you.

Exercise

Identify one or two clients who were satisfied working with you or your company.

Now reflect on:

- What problem did the client have before meeting you?
- How did you help them?
- What was the impact of working with you?

Summary

- ◇ Success stories are real-life examples of how a customer successfully used your product or service to solve a particular problem and achieve their desired outcomes

- ◇ The goal is to give your buyers confidence that you can solve their most crucial problems

- ◇ The best time to share a success story is when you have a very clear understanding of your buyers' pain points

Chapter 8

DIFFERENTIATION STORIES

"There are two questions that everybody has about you in every room, every day. 'Why you?' and 'Why now?' It doesn't matter if you're leading people, selling products, or raising capital."

– Craig Wortmann,
founder and Executive Director
of the Kellogg Sales Institute

Let's say you've had great conversations with your buyer. You've built a connection, asked the right questions to understand their situation, and shared an insightful story about a similar customer who you've worked with.

But before moving forward, there is one thing that the buyer needs to know: *why you?*

They might not ask you directly, but they're definitely thinking about it. This question can be asked in a lot of ways. Andy Paul,[7] author of *Sell without Selling Out*, lists a few:

- Why should I work with you?
- Why should I trust you?
- Why should I invest my time in you?
- Why should I collaborate with you?

They are slightly different questions, but they all come back to the core question:

Why you?

Inexperienced salespeople answer this question by listing all the great things about their company or themselves.

They'll say something like this, "We're the market leader in chemistry-free baby powder, we operate in 30 countries, and we invest 10% of our sales in R&D."

Well, these are important facts, and you should mention them at some point in your conversations. But think about it: are these facts enough to truly differentiate yourself? Do they answer the question "Why you?"

Most of the time, they don't. In the end, your buyer will hear very similar things from your competitors.

If you truly want to stand out, you need to share a story that shows how you're different: *a differentiation story.*

Differentiation stories are narratives that set you apart from your competitors, highlighting your unique value proposition and the benefits of doing business with you.

That is, unique in how you solve problems, how you support customers, or how you communicate. Really anything that is unique in your approach.

Let's look at two examples.

Example 1:

Storyteller: Mike Weinberg, author of *New Sales. Simplified.*

Point: I'll join your teams on the ground and won't shy away from the telling the (potentially uncomfortable) truth

> "In 2018, the CEO of a mid-sized company in the US hired us to train their sales teams to bring in more business. The CEO was a brilliant engineer. Extremely intelligent. He just didn't understand why nobody was selling.
>
> Two weeks into our partnership, I had the chance to participate in a quarterly meeting with the full company. Even though the company wasn't bringing in any new business, profits were at a record high.
>
> At the end of the meeting, the CEO said, 'Thank you, guys. Because of you, we've achieved the highest profits in the company's history.'
>
> Then he stood up, went around the room, and thanked each department individually. He thanked product, then engineering, then manufacturing, then operations. He even thanked facilities for the meals they were preparing every day.
>
> Do you know which department he didn't thank?
>
> Sales.

After participating in a few more meetings, I realized that the CEO didn't appreciate the salespeople. As an engineer, he wanted to give all the credit to product and engineering. Not to sales. He had created an anti-sales culture.

I told him about my observation, but he blamed the sales Vice President instead. I tried a few things to make him aware, but that wasn't too successful.

Six weeks into our partnership, I told the CEO 'Look, if you're not willing to look in the mirror, I can't work with you. If you want this training to amount to any long-term transformation, you need to change.' That day, I terminated our contract.

I care about results. When you work with me, I'll be very honest with you. There will be some things that you may not like. But if you truly want to transform your team's sales success, that's something you need to be OK with."

Example 2:

Storyteller: Thomas Gerber, director at a large pharma company in Europe

Point: We do everything in our capabilities to help out a customer

"It was June 2020 and we were 3 months into the global pandemic.

I was in my apartment in Zurich, about to finish my work when I got a call from one of our customers, the CEO of a large beauty clinic in Germany.

Very tense, he said, 'Thomas, this whole Covid thing is hitting us badly. Just a few months ago, we borrowed millions to open a new clinic. But now there is no business. We gotta cut our expenses and will have to end our contract with you."

Caught by surprise, I responded, 'Before you make a decision, give me a few days, OK? I'll try to figure something out for you.'

The moment I hung up, I started brainstorming with my team what we could do.

Quickly, I realized that we were all in no way prepared to deal with the pandemic. At least not here in Europe. But maybe in China, they were more prepared. What we were going through, they went through a month before.

And I thought, 'What if we connected our European clients with our Chinese clients?'

At first, I was skeptical because of potential compliance issues. Pharma is an extremely regulated market and bringing these companies together would be a major legal undertaking. But I also realized that we didn't have any other options. So I went for it.

Immediately, I set up an emergency working group consisting of eight people from legal, comms, ops, sales, and support.

Over the next few days, we talked to our customers in China, got all the legal approvals, hired translators, and outlined the session. Most of us completely ditched our day-to-day tasks to make it happen.

And it worked out. Two weeks later, one of our Chinese customers shared crisis best practices with our customers in Europe. They explained exactly what they'd done to deal with the pandemic, how to reduce costs, and how to still get some business in.

Immediately after the session, the CEO of the German company called me and said, 'Thomas, I loved the session. So many insights. You know, I was really thinking about cutting our partnership but what you guys did there showed me you're in it for the long run.'

That same customer managed to come out of the crisis very successfully and has actually been expanding across all of Europe. And we are happy to continue supporting the growth of his business."

How to find differentiation stories

First, think about what makes it unique to work with you. This unique claim could be, for instance, "I support your business at any hour, 365 days a year," "I'm a consultant to your business, not a salesperson," or "I care about my clients' long-term success."

Once you know what claim you want to make, find evidence to back it up. The evidence is any specific moment from your past that offers an example of when you lived that claim.

For instance, let's say your claim was "I care about my clients' long-term success." The evidence to back up that claim could be a moment where you recommended a client *not* to do a short-term investment, even though it would have given you far more sales.

Ask yourself: Is there a moment in your past where you:

- Went above and beyond to help your client?
- Tackled a problem in a unique way?
- Acted in an exemplary way?

How to deliver differentiation stories

Be different: If all of your competitors say "We put the customer first," this isn't going to help you differentiate yourself. Find something that the buyer cares about but also something that not everyone else is claiming. Otherwise, your story loses its power.

Be humble: Out of all the stories, this is where you toot your own horn the most. Be mindful not to brag too much and let the examples you chose speak for you. Sure, talk about what makes it so awesome to work with you, but also balance that with sharing something where you're maybe not so great. Be open to being vulnerable.

Exercise

1. Identify what makes it unique to work with you—a unique claim or value (e.g., "I always put the customer first" or "I don't shy away from the truth").

2. Identify one or two moments from your past that support this claim.

Summary

◇ Differentiation stories are narratives that set you apart from your competitors, highlighting your unique value proposition and the benefits of doing business with you

◇ The goal is to make your buyer understand why you are such a great fit for them

◇ The best time to bring in the story is when you talk about your company or your specific approach

Chapter 9

RESISTANCE STORIES

"Facts may inform, but stories transform."

– Brad Harmon,
sales executive at Oracle

Objections will come up. I know that there are some sales trainers who say, "If you buy my $6k course, you won't get any objections ever again in your life." Sure. And the moon is made of green cheese.

Even if you're the most skilled seller on the planet, you'll get pushback. It's inevitable and absolutely normal.

Your buyer may not be aligned with the price, your offer may not fit their current agenda, or something else.

In these moments, inexperienced sellers try to persuade the buyer with logic. They use arguments to tell the buyer why they should reconsider. They say something like, "You'll miss out on a massive opportunity. We can really help your business grow. Give us three months and we'll get rid of all of your manufacturing problems."

But, as you know, this approach is not very effective. It's tough to overcome any objections by using logic. Instead of trying to persuade someone with logic, try to appeal to their emotions instead. Use a story to overcome any objections: a *resistance story*.

Resistance stories are successful examples of customers who initially had doubts about working with you but ultimately decided to move forward and are now glad they did.

Let's look at two examples.

Example 1:

Storyteller: Mike Dutter, former VP of Sales at Oracle

Objection: No budget at the moment to buy the solution

Mike: "In June 2020, I met with the CMO of a large industrial manufacturing company. He was looking for a solution to help them segment their customers more effectively. Right when I thought it was a done deal, the CMO said, 'I like your solution, but to be honest, I don't see how we can justify that at the moment. Just last week, our CEO announced a "zero expenses" policy until the end of the fiscal year.' Similar constraints as you're seeing, right?"

Buyer: "Yes."

Mike: "Well, what we did was extend our meeting with the CMO by an hour and started brainstorming how we could make that happen. At the end of the meeting, we agreed that they could start using our technology already and pay the invoice six months later, in the new fiscal year. No interest, cost of funds, or similar. Is that something that could work for you?"

Buyer: "I guess this is something we could explore."

Mike: "Actually, by the time the customer made their first payment in the new fiscal year, the client had increased the revenue of the segmented customers by 300%. The additional revenue was $200k more than what they paid for the technology. How do you feel about such an arrangement? How far would that help you reach your goals?"

Example 2:

Storyteller: Mary Wheeler, sales executive at a large pharma company in US, selling doctors drugs to treat multiple sclerosis

Objection: Starting patients on drug samples takes too much time because of Food and Drug Administration (FDA) requirements

"About two years back, I talked to Dr Issa in New York about the possibility of starting patients on drug samples. Similar to you, he said, 'I'm not opposed to samples, but it's just too much work. It's not the good old times anymore. If I wanted to use more samples, I'd have to hire one person to do the admin.'

I said to him, 'Look, we know how samples can be pretty inconvenient for your team. So, we've started making some changes to make the process as simple and low effort as possible. Instead of getting dozens of samples, you get one sample, shipped from the company straight to your office. It's a tiny, refrigerated package. You don't have to track it, and you don't have to document it. Nothing.'

At first, Dr Issa was still a bit skeptical how we'd pull it off, but in the end he agreed to give it a try. He'd try using samples for a few months to see how much paperwork it actually was but also to see how effective the drug was.

From that moment onward, he received a tiny, refrigerated sample from us, every single week.

About ten months in, he gave me a call: 'Mary, it takes my MA [medical assistant] five minutes a week to log all the paperwork. But more importantly, not a single patient has had a relapse since starting with the samples. Thanks for nudging me on the samples.'

How about you? Would you be interested in starting on samples if there was barely any extra admin work involved?"

How to find resistance stories

First, become aware of the most common objections that you get. Go through your lost deals and review why you've lost these deals. Is it that you were too expensive, that the buyer didn't have the resources to start with your product, or that they didn't have the budget? Be very clear on that. It could be useful to review your transcripts and notes of your interactions to find what the objections are. Check in with your team to make sure you've identified the most relevant objections.

Once you're clear on the objections, start thinking about how you could use a story to respond to them. Review the deals you've closed that led to very satisfied customers and ask yourself:

- Did any of these customers have any objections or concerns initially?

- How did the situation turn out?

- What results did the customer achieve from working with you?

How to deliver resistance stories

Understand the objection: Do not jump into the story the moment the objection comes up. First, try to truly understand what's going on with your customer. Clarify what they mean by "your price is too high" or "let me think it over." You can ask questions like:

- "When you say … (repeat back what they said), what do you mean by that?"

- "I'm curious: why do you feel this way?"

- "Can you tell me what you mean by that exactly?"

Once you're clear on the objection, you can use a story that matches the buyer's concern. Otherwise, you risk sharing something that is not relevant and losing your buyer's attention.

Exercise

1. Identify the 2–3 most common objections you get.

2. Reflect on whether any of your satisfied clients had one of these objections initially.

3. For that specific client, reflect on:

   - What problem did the client have before meeting you?

   - How did you help them?

   - What was the impact of working with you?

Summary

◇ Resistance stories are success stories about customers who initially had doubts about working with you, but ultimately decided to move forward and are now glad they did

◇ The goal of these stories is to alleviate your buyer's concerns or objections when they arise

Bringing it together

Now we've covered the five crucial sales stories, let's quickly recap the focus and aim of each story type.

Story type	Focus	Goal
Connection stories	Something interesting that happened to you	Make buyers feel at ease
Industry stories	Challenges or trends in buyers' industry	Become buyers' trusted advisor
Success stories	Challenge that a buyer overcame with your help	Give buyers confidence that you can solve their problems
Differentiation stories	Experience that shows your unique approach	Stand out from the competition
Resistance stories	Challenge that an initially skeptical buyer overcame with your help	Alleviate buyers' concerns or objections

Chapter 10

ADDITIONAL TIPS TO FIND STORIES

"Great stories happen to those who can tell them."

– Ira Glass,
host of *This American Life*

While having one story for each of the five types is a great starting point, ideally you want to have a few variations for each type. For instance, one success story for each major customer segment, two differentiation stories for the qualities you want to highlight, and two resistance stories for the most prevalent objections.

By preparing 10–15 stories in total (2–3 variations of each story type), you'll be able to use stories in the most crucial moments of any sales conversation.

By now, you probably have plenty of experiences you could use as a story. But if you're struggling, no problem.

In this chapter, we'll look at 3 sources to identify experiences that could be turned into a story: 1) reviewing your experience, 2) interviewing customers, and 3) interviewing coworkers.

Source #1: Reviewing your experience

The easiest way to find stories is to review your own experience. This can be from your current role, your previous role, or even outside of work.

Take a look at your CRM, review all the deals you've closed, and try to recall how you helped your customers. Ask yourself:

1. What problem did the client have?
2. How did you help the client?
3. What was the impact of your product or service?

What you're looking for are situations that stand out—situations where you did something that set you apart from others, where you positively surprised your client, or where you helped your client achieve outstanding results.

Source #2: Interviewing customers

It may be easy to reflect on how you helped your customers, or it could be a bit harder. Why might it be harder? One reason could be that you don't have a systematic after-the-sale communication approach in place.

When I started my business, I didn't have an after-the-sale system in place. I rarely followed up with my clients after delivering my service. I had the mindset: 'Service delivered. Let's go and find more clients.' I didn't really check how they implemented what they had learned and what results they achieved from working with us. Without knowing that, it was impossible to craft powerful stories.

The moment I realized I was missing that information, I dropped my clients a quick note to see if they were free to hop on a 15-minute call. I wanted to understand the impact of my programs and coaching.

While I initially worried about being ignored, I was surprised when every single one of them got back to me. After chatting with dozens of clients, I had many more stories I could use.

And you can do the same. Just give some of your very satisfied clients a call. If your offer has helped them in any way, they'll be happy to talk to you.

So, what questions can you ask? Here are a few questions you could cover:

1. What was your experience with using our product (or service)?
2. How did our product (or service) help solve [original problem]?
3. What results have you achieved so far?
4. Was there anything that stood out when you worked with us?

The good thing is you have nothing to lose.

Outcome 1: Your client has unlocked massive results because of your help, giving you a great story.

Outcome 2: Your client hasn't got the desired results but gives you important feedback to refine your offering.

Either way, it's a win.

Source #3: Interviewing coworkers

Unless you work by yourself, there should be one or a few people in your company who you could reach out to for story ideas.

"Wait a second! I can tell a story that's not mine?" I hear you asking.

Absolutely.

It's easier to tell the story if it's your own, but if you struggle to come up with one, you can interview your coworker(s) to get more story ideas. No problem.

So, how can you get your coworkers to tell you their stories?

Let me walk you through the steps:

1. **Select people you'd like to interview**: This might be a seller who has been with your company for a few years, who has sold the products you're selling, and who is helpful. Or it might be someone who cares about your company and about other people, as they will be more than happy to help you. If you work for a start-up, you could interview one of the founders.

2. **Ask them for an interview**: Once you've identified who you'd like to talk to, just drop them a quick note. Don't overthink it. It should be enough to say, "Do you have 30 minutes to talk about your experience? I'd like to gather a few examples of how you've helped some of our clients. No prep needed." People love talking about their experience and will be proud that you've chosen them.

3. **Ask them about their experience**: After giving some context, it's time to move on to the actual interview. Let's start off with what you should avoid at any cost, which includes questions like "So, do you have a great story that I could use?" or "Tell me your story."

Why? Well, it puts immense pressure on your interviewee. Most people don't think of their experiences as stories. So, if you ask them for their story, they will likely feel overwhelmed. It's too vague and too broad. It's better to approach your interview like a conversation where you ask them a bunch of questions.

Here are some questions you could ask:

1. Can you tell me about a specific customer who was very happy using our products/services?

2. Do you remember how they got in touch with you?

3. What was their situation like before they began working with you? What problems were they going through? How did they feel?

4. How did you help them?

5. How did your solution change their situation? How did they feel after solving that problem?

If you hear any stories you'd like to use, ask the person for their permission to use the story in your conversations. Check whether you can use the actual client names or whether you should tell the story without disclosing any names.

Saving your stories

By now, you're starting to gather more and more ideas that could be turned into great stories.

To make sure you don't rely on your brain to remember all of these, it's helpful to store your stories in a central place called the *Story Bank*.

The Story Bank is a central place to capture, classify, and remember your stories.

You can use any medium or technology to save your stories as long as it doesn't add too much friction. You can save your stories electronically (e.g., Evernote, Google Docs, Notion, or Word) or on paper (e.g., journal). I prefer to store them electronically in Google Docs as it allows me to find the stories easily, edit them, and access them wherever I am. But I'd encourage you to pick the medium that you feel most comfortable with.

What information should you capture in the Story Bank?

Here's the information I capture:

- **Title**: A short title that allows you to easily remember the story
- **Use case**: Situations you could use the story in
- **Audience**: The audience you can share the story with
- **Point**: The point of the story (a story can have multiple points)
- **Story type**: The type of story (e.g., success story)
- **Source**: The place where you discovered the story
- **Summary**: Bullets that will help you remember the story (instead of writing full sentences, focus on short bullets)

To give you an idea of how this looks in real life, here's Luke's summarized story (from Chapter 2):

Title	Preventing future hair loss
Use case	When learning that the prospect spends lots of time to pay contractors
Audience	Accounting managers
Point	Deel saves you time and helps you scale the business
Story type	Success story
Source	Own story
Summary	**Context**: In April 2021, sales call with an Accounting manager at a US-based online study platform. **Challenge**: Client says, "I'm gonna be bold. I'm literally pulling out my hair right now." Spends a full week each month paying contractors via PayPal, etc. Big problem as they plan to increase number of contractors from 400 to 900. **Response**: Within 10 days, onboarded 400 existing contractors on Deel, giving client time to onboard the 500 new contractors. **Result**: Client calls and says, "Before, it took me a week to get through the contractor payroll. Now, it takes me less than an hour. This was game-changing!"

Story Bank

Do you want to save yourself time and not create a Story Bank from scratch? Go to power-of-storytelling.com/kit and download the Story Bank template for free. The template is available for Google Docs.

Exercise

Pick one of the three strategies (reviewing your experience, interviewing customers, or interviewing coworkers) and gather additional story ideas.

Summary

◇ You can identify experiences that can be turned into a story by 1) reviewing your past experience, 2) interviewing customers, or 3) interviewing coworkers

◇ Look for any situations that stand out or set you apart from others

◇ Once you've found a story that stands out, outline the story and save it to your Story Bank

PART 3

BUILD
CONFIDENCE

Beginner storytellers often feel insecure about sharing a story in front of an audience. They may feel that their story isn't good enough, that it needs to be perfect, or that it's not the right time.

Expert storytellers jump at every opportunity to tell stories, and they feel comfortable doing so. They don't wait for their stories to be perfect, but instead embrace imperfection.

In Part 3, you'll learn how to practice your stories, overcome any self-limiting beliefs holding you back, and visualize using stories effectively.

Should you still read this part if you already feel pretty confident?

For me, building confidence is a lifelong journey. Even though I feel confident today, I know that every tiny improvement in my confidence brings more bliss and helps me go after any goal I set for myself. So yes, even if you feel pretty confident, I suggest checking it out.

Chapter 11

PRACTICE STORIES

"Get the story on paper, say it out loud, make edits, and test it in a non-sales environment. Once your friends understand it and find that the story serves your purpose, you're ready to share it in your sales conversations."

– Lee B. Salz,
author of *Sell Different!*

By now, you know how to structure, enhance, and simplify your stories. If you had planned to focus on written storytelling, we could have stopped here.

But as our focus is on oral storytelling, we have to make sure the story *sounds* as good as it reads. So in this chapter, you'll learn how to practice your story out loud.

Let's start with what you *shouldn't* do.

Don'ts

1. Don't try to "wing it"

Some people prefer not to rehearse their story so it appears more natural when they tell it. While I like the idea behind this, I wouldn't recommend it. By not rehearsing at all, there's a strong chance that you'll talk too much about information that doesn't matter or miss crucial moments of the story.

By winging it, you're setting yourself up for average results. Like in any other discipline, if you want outstanding results, you have to put in the reps.

2. Don't rehearse in your head only

Often, we rehearse our stories and presentations by *thinking* about what we want to say. This is a risky strategy. By only thinking about it, you won't know how long the story is, how to use your voice and body to support the story, and how to pronounce certain words correctly.

3. Don't rehearse in front of a mirror

Every time I hear the tip "rehearse in front of a mirror," I'm shocked how anyone can give that advice. When will you ever be in a situation telling a story while also seeing yourself?

Never! It's completely unnatural to see yourself while speaking. Even for online meetings, you should look at your listener or into the camera instead of looking at yourself. The only thing you accomplish by looking at yourself is that you get more self-conscious about how you look.

Now we're clear on what you shouldn't do, let's talk about what you can do instead.

Do's

1. Do rehearse your story 2–4 times

While the number of times you rehearse depends on your learning style, I've noticed that most of my clients rehearse their stories 2–4 times to feel comfortable sharing them in front of an audience that matters (e.g., a client or coworker). Rehearsing 2–4 times is not enough to remember every single line of the story, but it's enough to remember the most crucial moments and experiences of the story. This way, the story will still sound natural.

2. Do rehearse speaking out loud

Rehearse your story in the same way you'll be delivering it: by speaking out loud. Speak as if you were sharing the story with an actual audience. Use the same volume, pace, and pauses you'd use in real life. This way, your delivery won't change when it matters. When you mess up, don't stop your story or start from the beginning. Try to go on. In doing so, you'll train your mind to deal with any problems that arise.

3. Do practice with a buddy

Find someone who knows how to give feedback, has time to help you, and ideally knows a little bit about storytelling (though the last bit is optional).

In the session, share your story and ask them what they liked about it and what could be improved. A third-party perspective is extremely helpful in understanding how the story plays out in real life.

I often call my sisters or close friends to get feedback on my stories. They are not storytelling experts. But they can tell me whether they understood the point of the story, if they got lost somewhere, and how the story made them feel. Often, the first versions of my stories are as thrilling as a lecture on tax law. But by getting this outside perspective, I'm able to drastically improve my stories.

4. Do speak in front of an imaginary audience

In sales, you may not have a mega-large audience in one room all that often. More than likely, it's just one other person. Whether it's a one-to-one conversation or more people, eye contact is incredibly important. Deliberate eye contact builds trust, signals confidence, and gives you feedback on how your story is landing.

How can you practice having deliberate eye contact?

By using the objects in your room as the audience. For instance, your plant is one person, your photo frame is another person, and your pet spider is another one.

When you share your story, rest your eyes on one object for a full sentence or thought, then then move on to the next object. It feels a little awkward at the beginning, but it's a great way to practice deliberate eye contact.

5. Do record yourself

Recording yourself is a tough one, I gotta admit. After years of doing it, I still cringe seeing myself. But it is a super useful technique. So don't skip it.

While you don't have to record every single story, it can be good practice to record yourself on camera once in a while. Just hit the record button and look directly into the camera. Don't look at your own image as it will distract you and make you more self-conscious.

The objective is to spot any behaviors that are *not* helping your story. For instance, did you rush through your story, did you sound monotone, or did you look grumpy while telling your story? My default facial expression used to be close to that of a moody, puberty-hitting teenager. So I had to make a deliberate effort to remind myself every single time to look friendlier when I shared a story.

What about body language?

In my programs, I'm often asked whether I have any tips on how to improve your body language.

My response in most cases is the same, "Don't worry about it."

The moment you start thinking something like "Let me raise my arm here to highlight the increase in revenue," it's likely going to look fake. I prefer to see the story in front of my eyes and feel the emotions of the story. By doing that, I'll automatically use the body language that fits the story.

When perfection matters

For most sales conversations, your story doesn't have to be perfect. It should be enough to rehearse it a few times using the techniques we've just explored.

But for certain high-stake meetings, you may want to know every single line by heart. For instance, when you try to close the largest account in your region or when the next deal should result in your promotion.

Let me share an example of how I prepared for an event where every single word mattered.

In May 2022, I got a call from an anonymous number.

"Hi Philipp, this is Mike from TEDx Roermond. I don't want to talk about fate, but we had a speaker drop out. With that, we have a spot open. Are you interested?"

"Ahh, sure. When is it?"

"It's next Wednesday."

"You mean, Wednesday in 6 days?"

"Yeah. I know it's tight. Are you up for it?"

For the previous 7 years, I'd been dreaming about giving a TED talk. As someone eternally lost in a midlife crisis, I've watched an unhealthy amount of TED talks.

This was my chance.

In a rather high-pitched voice, I said, "Yeah. I'm up for it."

For the next 6 days, I spent 10 hours every day writing, revising, visualizing, and rehearsing my talk. I applied rehearsal techniques that I had learned in acting classes in the previous years.

First, I spoke my script in different voices (e.g., as if I were an old English lady or an Aussie surfer boy), making it easier to remember.

Second, I rehearsed my talk while walking in the street (feeling the judgment of other people).

Third, I visualized the worst thing that could happen: pooping my pants on stage. After six *shitty* visualizations, I realized 'yeah that would suck, but I could probably deal with it.'

So, 6 days later, it was game time. I delivered my TED talk in front of hundreds of people.

Within 24 hours of being on YouTube, my TED talk had been watched by 40k people.

The same day, the global TED organization selected my talk out of hundreds of other talks as their "Editor's Pick."

The dream that I'd been fantasizing about for years came true within *one week*.

***

Curious about the talk?

You can check it out here:

https://www.youtube.com/watch?v=3tj2VxXfARk

Exercise

Let's go back to the story that you've been working on and start practicing it.

Find a room where you won't be disturbed. Stand up and say your story out loud two to three times or however long it takes you to feel comfortable. Feel free to move your eye contact deliberately from one object to another, and record your story.

Summary

◇ Confidence comes from honing and perfecting your skills through practice

◇ Don't try to wing it or just *think* about the parts of your story

◇ Instead, share your stories a few times, out loud, ideally in front of someone who can give you feedback

Chapter 12

OVERCOME YOUR SELF-LIMITING BELIEFS

"If we can see past preconceived limitations, then the possibilities are endless."

– Amy Purdy,
actress, para-snowboarder,
and author of *On My Own Two Feet*

Let's start with a quick analogy about an elephant at a circus.

The elephant is the strongest animal in the circus. But while all the other animals are held in cages, the elephant is only tied to a rope—a rope that the elephant could easily break.

So, what is preventing them from breaking free?

Well, at a young age, the elephant was tied to a rope. At that age, the elephant tried to break free many times. But at that point, they couldn't. With each failed attempt, they started to believe they weren't strong enough. After trying multiple times, they stopped trying.

A few years later, they have grown into a big and powerful animal but still believe they're not strong enough. The elephant has been conditioned to believe they can't break away. These beliefs are holding the elephant back.

Now, why am I sharing this example? Well, the same applies to us as humans.

We all have negative thoughts about ourselves, our abilities, or our future. Often, these thoughts hold us back from taking risks, reaching our goals, and achieving our full potential.

Let me share an example from one of my clients.

In April 2021, I hopped on a coaching call with Esraa, a customer success manager from Canada. On the call, I was greeted by a bundle of energy. Esraa is a very extroverted and charismatic woman.

Immediately, I asked myself "How can I help her? She should be coaching me and not the other way around. I've probably got to tell her that I can't help." But keeping these thoughts to myself, I asked her a few questions.

A couple of minutes in, I asked her to share a story she had prepared.

The moment I asked her to share the story, her entire energy changed. That big bundle of energy shrank to an insecure pile of misery. She looked down, bit her bottom lip, and let out a long 'ahhhhh.'

After she told her story, I asked, "Esraa, what just happened? You have this incredible presence, but the moment you started your story, it just disappeared. What's going on?"

She replied, "I don't know. Somehow, I'm scared that people will make fun of me and that I'm not articulate enough."

I asked her a few more questions to find out what was going on. It turned out that she had struggled a lot when she moved from Iraq to Canada when she was 12 years old. For years, she felt that people made fun of her English. Now, she felt comfortable in normal situations, but in higher stake situations, she freaked out.

Like the example from earlier, when I saw this, I knew there was no point working on story structure or elements. We had to work on overcoming her self-limiting beliefs.

For the next hour, we looked at the things she had been telling herself, where they came from, and how we could reframe them. In that one hour, we essentially rewrote her story.

At the end of our session, I asked her to tell the story a second time. When she finished, I looked at her in awe and said, "Wow, Esraa. You're a phenomenal storyteller. What a transformation."

At that point, she broke down in tears saying, "Philipp, thank you so much. Thinking I'm not articulate enough has been holding me back for years. Now, I know it doesn't have to be part of my identity. Thank you."

Esraa's self-limiting belief was that her English wasn't good enough. For you, it could be something completely different. Let's find out what belief has been holding you back and how you can overcome it to reach your full potential.

Step 1: Identify the self-limiting belief

The first step is to identify your self-limiting beliefs. What have you been telling yourself all these years that is holding you back?

These self-limiting beliefs can be specifically about your storytelling or public speaking skills, or your overall confidence and self-worth.

Here are a few common self-limiting beliefs that many of my clients have nurtured:

- I'm a terrible storyteller
- My English is not good enough
- My face turns red when I start sharing a story
- I don't have any interesting stories
- My stories are not good enough
- I'm not smart enough
- I'm boring

Become aware of them. Any of these beliefs may impact your ability to tell great stories.

Step 2: Challenge the belief

Once you've identified a self-limiting belief, it's time to challenge it. Ask yourself whether the belief is actually true. Is there evidence to support it, or is it just a thought you've repeated to yourself so many times that it feels true?

By evidence, we're not talking about your inner thoughts but *external* data points. For example, did a friend tell you that you're a terrible storyteller? Or did your manager say you aren't smart enough? If it's based on mere conjecture and not facts (hint: most likely, it's not), it's time to put this belief behind you.

Questions to challenge the belief:

- Is this belief really grounded in reality? What are the supporting facts?
- Did I always think this way?
- If not, what has changed?
- Is there evidence that goes against my belief?

Step 3: Consider the consequences

In the next step, become aware of the implications of this belief. What will you miss out on in life if you do *not* change this belief? Also, what will you gain in life by changing this belief?

The more you can become aware of both scenarios, the more urgency you'll have to adopt a new belief system.

Ask yourself:

- How is this belief serving me?

- How will *not* changing this belief affect me in the long term (relationships, career, happiness, etc.)?

- How would my life look in 3, 6, 12 months if I didn't have this belief?

Step 4: Replace the belief

In the next step, replace your old belief with a new, more positive belief. Pick an alternative belief that sounds authentic to you. Otherwise, it may not be as effective.

Let's say your negative belief is "I'm a terrible storyteller." Saying "I'm the greatest storyteller on earth" may feel a bit too much. Your brain may not be fooled that easily. It would make more sense to say, "I may not be the best storyteller *yet*, but I've got a few cool stories to tell."

Or if, for instance, your negative belief is "My English is not good enough," a more productive belief could be "My English may not be perfect *yet*, but no one really cares if it's perfect. In fact, the easier I speak, the more impactful my story will be."

I'm sure you noticed that each example includes a *yet*. Yet is a powerful word that will help you accept your current situation but also give you faith that eventually you'll reach your full potential.

Step 5: Put the new belief into practice

The last step is to test the new belief in real life. If your new belief is "I may not be the best storyteller yet but I've a few cool stories," go ahead and commit to taking some low-risk actions to test the new belief. For instance, you could tell your friend or partner about your day, using outer dialogue or inner dialogue. There's no need to tell a full story but instead take small actions to test the new belief.

It's important to remember that replacing a self-limiting belief won't happen overnight. It takes time and effort to change the way you think. Most of my clients review and replace any self-limiting beliefs regularly over an extended period of a few months. Yes, it takes time, but it's a path worth taking. With practice, you'll see a true change in your belief system and you'll be able to pursue any goal in life.

Exercise

Let's start rewriting the stories you tell yourself by going through the following steps:

1. **Identify the self-limiting belief**: Pick a few beliefs that have negatively impacted your confidence or ability to tell stories.

2. **Challenge the belief**: Pick one belief and ask yourself: "Is this belief really grounded?" and "What are the supporting facts?"

3. **Consider the consequences**: Ask yourself: "What will my life be like in the future if 1) I continue with that belief or 2) I let go of that belief?"

4. **Replace the belief**: Replace the belief with a new, more constructive belief.

5. **Put the new belief into practice**: Commit to one small action today to test the new belief.

⬡ **Summary**

◇ We tell ourselves stories all the time. But often, the stories we tell ourselves hurt our confidence and our ability to tell better stories

◇ You can take control of the narrative by identifying your self-limiting beliefs, challenging the beliefs, considering the consequences, replacing them with an alternative belief, and putting the new beliefs into practice

Chapter 13

VISUALIZE THE FUTURE

"If you want to reach a goal, you must 'see the reaching' in your own mind before you actually arrive at your goal."

– Zig Ziglar

In 2000, 22-year-old Laura Wilkinson was invited to participate at the Olympic Games in platform diving. This was a big moment for her. It had been her dream since she was a little girl and may have been her only shot.[12]

Around 6 months before the Olympic Games, she was at the pool practicing her jumps.

But in one of the jumps, something went wrong. Instead of landing in the water directly, her feet hit the wooden block that she was jumping off. "Craaack."

Feeling a sharp pain in her right foot, she immediately knew that something was wrong.

Shortly after, the doctor confirmed that she had 3 broken bones in her right foot. Only 6 months before the Olympic Games.

At that point, most of us would probably have given up. But not Laura. After processing the initial shock, she resumed her practice. Well, not the usual physical practice, as she couldn't jump. Instead, she practiced mentally.

Every day, she spent hours visualizing every detail of her jumps at the Olympic Games. She imagined climbing up onto the diving board, preparing for her jump, and completing the jump perfectly. She even imagined climbing out of the pool.

Fast forward 6 months and she was at the Olympic Games in Sydney, standing on top of the diving board, wearing a protective shoe around her broken foot. Her foot still hurt, but that didn't stop her.

Three rounds later, she had done the unthinkable.

She won the gold medal in platform diving. She was the first American woman to win the gold medal in platform diving since 1964. An incredible achievement!

Laura is just one example of how visualization or mental imagery can be used to achieve peak performance. Many successful business people, actors, and performers (including Oprah Winfrey, Ed Mylett, Pete Carroll, and Michael Jordan) use visualization as a technique to feel more confident.

But how can visualization help you feel more confident telling stories in sales conversations?

By visualizing yourself using stories successfully, you'll:

1. Feel less anxious and more at ease as you've already told the story multiple times in your head.

2. Overcome any self-limiting beliefs by already experiencing the desired outcome.

3. Build positive associations and emotions around storytelling as your brain will associate stories with happy customers.

Let's say you have an important meeting coming up and you'd like to use stories to influence the outcome of the meeting—here are the steps you can take to visualize the event:

Step 1: Set a goal

Set a specific goal for telling the story. What do you want to accomplish with the story? For example, you may want to show what is unique about working with you, inspire your buyer to take a certain action, or just build a connection with them.

Step 2: Get into a relaxed state

Choose a comfortable place where you won't be interrupted. This can be a chair, couch, bed, or anywhere you feel relaxed and at ease.

Close your eyes and take a few deep breaths to relax and clear your mind.

Breathe in through your nose. While breathing in, let your belly expand. Make sure that your chest is *not* expanding, remaining as still as possible.

Then, breathe out slowly through your mouth, pursing your lips together as if you were going to whistle (or making the sound of a balloon losing air). While breathing out, let your belly move inward.

After breathing like this 5 to 10 times, you will feel significantly more grounded, present, and relaxed.

Step 3: Visualize the event

In the next step, use your imagination to create a clear mental picture of a specific event that will help you reach your goal. If, for instance, your goal is to "close the deal", imagine having a meeting with the buyer and using a story to close the deal. Imagine the details of the event, including the:

- Setting of the meeting (room layout, furniture, lighting)
- Person you're telling the story to (height, build, clothes)
- Telling of the story (feeling confident, smooth delivery, friendly audience)
- Outcome of telling the story ("win" moment, sense of satisfaction, feeling confident)

Try to make your visualization as vivid and realistic as possible. The more details you can imagine and the more you can feel your emotions, the more effective the exercise will be.

Let's make it more concrete.

Here's a sample visualization script you can use to feel more confident to deliver your stories in a sales conversation.

Sample visualization script

Close your eyes and take a few deep breaths to relax and clear your mind.

Visualize the scene where you're telling the story. That can be at the buyer's office, in a video conference, or anywhere else.

Notice the details of the room, such as the layout, furniture, and the lighting.

Notice how your buyer looks, observing their height, build, hair style, clothing, and any distinguishing marks.

You feel excited to share your story.

As you go into your story, notice the buyer looking at you with a relaxed and friendly face.

Visualize yourself owning the story. You love telling it.

Notice how you bring in some of the elements such as surprise or emotions to keep them interested.

And notice how it's working. They hang on to every word you say.

As you continue telling the story, feel the sense of joy and fulfillment it brings to you.

Imagine the buyer responding positively to your story, nodding, smiling, asking questions, and showing appreciation.

Finally, visualize the amazing outcome of the meeting.

Imagine the buyer telling you that they loved your story.

They want to partner with you and they thank you for sharing the story.

Feel the sense of achievement and satisfaction that comes from achieving your goal. Thank yourself for using stories so effectively.

Take a few more deep breaths and slowly open your eyes.

Note that the script focused on a meeting with your buyer. But to be clear, you can use visualization for any important meeting. I use visualization before giving an important presentation, jumping on a call with a buyer, or going to some anxiety-inducing social gathering.

Visualizing for roughly 5–10 minutes will get you in a very confident state.

To see a lasting change in confidence, it's helpful to repeat the visualization exercise a few times, adding more details and refining your visualization skills each time. It takes some time to get good at visualizing the details, but it's totally worth the effort.

Exercise

Pick an upcoming meeting or presentation that matters and visualize using stories to reach your goal.

Try to really see the event unfold in your mind. The more details you can imagine and the more emotions you can feel, the more fruitful the exercise will be.

Summary

◇ Visualization is a powerful tool to build long-term confidence and help you feel excited to share stories in your sales conversations

◇ To visualize effectively, it's good to 1) set the goal for telling the story, 2) get into a relaxed state, and 3) visualize the event in great detail

◇ The more specific, detailed, and emotionally involved you can get in your visualization, the more you'll benefit from it

Bonus tip: constructive embarrassment

Are you looking to drastically increase your confidence? Are you willing to try out some less conventional techniques?

One technique that I love but is not for everyone (thus why it's not included earlier) is *constructive embarrassment.*

Constructive embarrassment is a practice where you put yourself in an uncomfortable or embarrassing situation—on purpose.

This can be anything that is embarrassing to you, such as asking a stranger for a high five, singing in the street, or doing yoga poses in the supermarket.

I know what you're thinking... "Why would I do that? I've done enough embarrassing things in my life!"

Well, if you can handle feelings of shame in those situations, you can handle those feelings in any situation. You'll no longer obsessively care about what other people think. You'll get comfortable sharing your story in front of any audience. And you'll build the belief that everything in life turns out fine.

But don't worry that you'll need to start with the hardest activities straight away. You can start small by asking a stranger for directions, asking a stranger for a hug, or giving a stranger a compliment. Any small situation where your first reaction is "Nah, that's awkward" is a great opportunity to embarrass yourself.

Curious to find out more? You can check my TEDx talk on constructive embarrassment: https://www.youtube.com/watch?v=3tj2VxXfARk

PART 4

DELIVER STORIES

Beginner storytellers often struggle to weave stories into their conversations. They may not find the right time to deliver the story, might tell a story that is not relevant to their audience, or may go into performance mode so the delivery feels inauthentic.

Expert storytellers know how to weave the right story into the conversation as naturally as possible. They prepare by researching their audience and tailoring their stories to each situation.

In Part 4, you'll learn how to prepare for your conversations, get your buyers to open up, and transition in and out of your stories smoothly.

Chapter 14

TAILOR YOUR STORIES

"By failing to prepare, you are preparing to fail."

– Benjamin Franklin

In 2022, LinkedIn[8] found that 4 out of 5 sellers (82%) who exceeded their quota by 50% or more said they did research "all of the time" before reaching out to prospects.

You cannot plan for everything but you can increase your chances of having your stories land well by doing some thorough pre-meeting planning.

Let me walk you through the steps you can take before meeting a buyer.

Step 1: Understand your audience

The first step is to get a clear picture of the person you're about to meet. If you don't know them, take a quick look on LinkedIn. This will tell you what company they work for, what the company does, how big the company is, what industry they're in, how long they've been with their current company, what education they have, and what they're interested in.

While this may all seem like basic information at first, these are all data points that will help you craft or select a story that is relevant to them.

Let's look at an example. Imagine your job is to sell CRM software to enterprise clients. In a few days, you have a meeting with the Head of Purchasing at an eyewear distribution company. You go on LinkedIn to find out more about the individual and the company. After a few clicks, you've gathered the following information:

Buyer information:

- *Name:* Sam Fenwick
- *Role:* Head of Tech Purchasing
- *Time in company:* 10 years
- *Education:* MBA at Kellogg
- *Interests:* Follows Satya Nadella (CEO of Microsoft) and Tim Ferris (motivational speaker), is part of the Kellogg Debate Society and the Sustainability Group

Company information:

- *Company scope:* Designs, manufactures, and distributes eyewear (glasses and sunglasses) to opticians
- *Company size:* 1.3k employees
- *Industry:* Retail apparel or fashion

Researching your buyer takes less than 5 minutes but it is key in selecting stories that are relevant to them.

Step 2: Define the goal for the meeting

Once you're clear on your audience, ask yourself, "What do I want my buyer to think, feel, and do?"

	Reflection	Examples
Think	What do you want your buyer to think after listening to your story?	• That you put your customers' problems above anything else • That you offer 10x more value than your competitor
Feel	What emotion do you want to evoke with your story?	• Hopeful • Excited
Do	What specific action do you want your audience to take?	• Buy your product • Share your pitch with management

If we go back to our previous example of selling a CRM to an eyewear distributor, the goal of the meeting might be this:

- **Think**: Our CRM software can help you increase sales by 20%

- **Feel**: Excited

- **Do**: Be invited to pitch the CRM to the CEO

Once you're clear on your audience and what you want to get out of the meeting, you can prepare a story that will help you reach that goal.

Step 3: Prepare a relevant story

In the last step, prepare any stories you could use to reach the meeting's goals. Usually, I don't prepare a story for each of the five story types but instead prepare one to three stories that could potentially work for that buyer. I don't know whether I'll be able to use the stories I've prepared but by having more stories ready, I'm increasing my chances that one of the stories is relevant to my buyer.

First, use the buyer's education and interests to pick a connection story that could be relevant to them. As Sam (our fictional character) is following Tim Ferriss, chances are high that he has some interest in personal development. Hence, you could prepare a quick connection story about a recent skill you learned and ask whether he's learned any cool skills in the last 6 months.

Second, use the company information to prepare an industry story. What challenges have you noticed when working with other retail companies? Any challenges, trends, or new technologies that are impacting their businesses? If you haven't worked with any companies in the space, go on Google and search for keywords such as "eyewear distribution trends" or "challenges in the retail industry." Spend 5 minutes browsing the first articles, but if you don't find anything, don't worry about it. Just skip the industry story.

Third, use the company information to pick a success story that is relevant to your buyer. Ideally, you're looking for another customer with a similar scope (e.g., eyewear distribution).

But as this can be challenging, it's OK to pick someone in a similar industry (e.g., retail) and with a comparable company size (e.g., 1k–5k employees).

Fourth, as you want your buyer to know that you can help them increase sales by 20%, you could prepare a differentiation story that proves the point. This could be a story about a time you offered another customer a success guarantee.

Lastly, you can use the industry information to anticipate any objections. If you've had a few customers in retail, you'll know they are under immense cost pressures and they'll always push back on price. For this, you could prepare a resistance story about another customer who initially pushed back on price but recovered their investment after 2 months.

Review your Story Bank to see whether there are any stories you could use. If there is nothing there, review your list of clients and see whether you have any experience that could serve as a story.

Exercise

Pick an upcoming meeting with a buyer and:

1. Understand who your buyer is (e.g., company, industry, interests, etc.)

2. Define the meeting goals (what you want the buyer to think, feel, and do)

3. Prepare one story that could help you reach your goals

⬦ **Summary** ⬦

⬧ To use the right story for the right audience, you need to do some proper pre-meeting planning

⬧ A quick online search will help you prepare a story that is aligned with your meeting goal and relevant to your buyer

⬧ Prepare one to three relevant stories before a meeting to increase your chances of using stories effectively

Chapter 15

LISTEN TO UNDERSTAND

"Imagine you tell me a story of your recent vacation. How incredible it was and how much fun you had. But instead of listening, I sit there thinking about my previous vacations. The second you stop, I immediately jump in with my story. What would you think? You'd think, 'why did I even tell that story, right?'"

– Scott Ingram,
Account Director at Relationship One

In 2016, Gong Revenue Intelligence[9] set out on a quest to understand what sets the top-performing sales reps apart from other sales reps, by analyzing the data of roughly 25k B2B sales conversations using AI. They found that the **top sales reps listen 23% more than the bottom sales reps.**

The top reps talked on average 43% and listened 57%, while the bottom reps talked 66% and listened 34%.

Fascinating, right? There's a correlation between how successful you are in sales and your ability to listen. Listening helps you build trust, improve problem solving, and defuse any objections. But why does it matter for the stories you tell?

Because before telling any story, you need to have a great understanding of what's going on in your client's business, what they're struggling with, and what they'd like to accomplish in the future. You want to uncover what truly matters to your buyer.

Once you know that, you can select a story that is relevant to your buyer, like a story about another customer who experienced similar struggles. By knowing what the buyer wants, you can tailor your story to highlight what matters to them.

How can you get to the core of what matters to the buyer? By listening to understand.

Listening to understand means listening with your whole self—giving your undivided attention both intellectually and emotionally.

Here are five techniques to help you listen to understand:

1. Ground yourself

Your days are probably packed with back-to-back meetings. You jump from one meeting to another without a minute in between. And even though you'd like to listen to the other person, your mind is still processing information from the previous meeting. How can you avoid this?

By grounding yourself through your breathing.

Take 1–2 minutes before a meeting to breathe deeply. Notice your feet on the ground and tune into how you feel in this specific moment.

It helps to set your meetings to 25 minutes by default (instead of 30 minutes) or 55 minutes (instead of 60 minutes) so you have enough time to grab a coffee, go to the restroom if you need to, and ground yourself.

2. Set your intention

Go into the meeting with the intention to understand what's really going on with the other person. Often, I tell myself, **"I'm gonna listen as if I were freaking Oprah Winfrey,"** "I'm gonna listen to her as if she is the most interesting person on earth," or "I'm gonna find out what truly matters to that person." Just by saying this to myself once or twice, I'm more likely to make it my reality.

3. Hold the silence

Instead of jumping into your solution the moment the buyer stops talking (aka premature elaboration), wait 1–3 seconds before you respond.

This way, you give your buyer space to go deeper into what truly matters to them. By holding the silence, you also signal that you're processing the information that they have given you.

As a heads-up, this feels extremely uncomfortable at first. All our life, we've been conditioned to avoid any moment of silence, so we anxiously jump in to fill the space.

Try to move away from this thinking and experiment with holding the silence. Hold it for 1–3 seconds after the other person has finished their thought. It will be tough at the beginning but will feel less awkward after a few times. Guaranteed.

4. Ask clarifying questions

Instead of jumping from one question or topic to another, try to go deeper into what the buyer has told you. The moment they share something important, ask them clarifying questions. Here are my favorite questions:

- "Can you tell me more about that?"

- "Can you explain that? I want to make sure I understand you correctly."

- "Why do you think that is the case?"

Asking these questions will give you a deeper understanding of what is truly going on. It also signals that you're really interested in what they are telling you.

5. Paraphrase what you've heard

Not only do you want to signal that you're listening, but you want to signal that you've understood them. You want your listener to feel, 'wow, they really get me.' You can do this by paraphrasing what you've just heard.

Here are some phrases you can use:

- "What I hear from you is… Is that right?"

- "Sounds like you are saying… Did I get that right?"

- "If I'm hearing you correctly…"

- "That must have been very… for you."

Note that we're not only paraphrasing but also acknowledging their emotion and asking them to confirm (e.g., "Is that right?" and "Is that correct?"). This shows that you empathize with their situation and allows you to confirm whether you got it right. If you misunderstood your buyer, it's better to be aware early rather than sharing a story that isn't relevant to them.

The good thing with listening is that you can practice it anywhere and every day.

You don't need to wait for that one important meeting with the buyer. You can practice listening anytime with your coworkers, friends, or family. Sure, you may have heard your grandmother's story a gazillion times already, but maybe this time you'll learn something absolutely fascinating (Grandma: in the unlikely event that you learned English and you're reading my book, please know that I love your stories).

But let's bring it back to your sales meetings. In the meeting, you want to listen to find out what's really going on with your buyer. Once you're crystal clear on the buyer's pain points and goals, you can share a story that is relevant to your buyer. Maybe this story is one you prepared as part of the pre-meeting planning, or maybe not. Be flexible to share a story that fits your buyer's needs.

Exercise

In an upcoming conversation, try listening to understand. This can be at work or outside of work. Go ahead and try to apply a few of the techniques we've just covered:

1. Ground yourself.

2. Set an intention.

3. Hold the silence.

4. Ask clarifying questions.

5. Paraphrase what you've heard.

Don't worry if you don't apply all five techniques straight away. This usually takes quite some practice. Even if you apply just one of the techniques, you're a much better listener already.

―――――――――――――――⟨ **Summary** ⟩―――――――――――――

⬦ Top-performing sales reps spend much more time listening than the bottom ones

⬦ Listening to understand means listening with your undivided attention

⬦ Great listening helps to build rapport, but also to pick a story that is relevant to your buyer's struggles

Chapter 16

SHARE YOUR STORY

"A great story is a conversation and not a presentation. It's not an 18-minute TED talk. It's about uncovering the buyer's challenges, sharing a few challenges that you've seen somewhere else, asking buyers how these relate to their challenges and sharing how others have overcome these challenges."

– Mike Weinberg,
author of *New Sales. Simplified.*

StorySelling is exchanging dialogue.

You're *not* expected to give a 5-minute monologue. That's 'big storytelling,' which is helpful for keynotes, all-hands, and other leadership announcements but *not* for 99% of sales conversations.

If you want to connect with your buyer, you have to weave your stories into your conversation. In this chapter, you'll learn how.

Step 1: Transition in

So, you've uncovered your buyer's main pain points and you're ready to share a story.

How can you transition into your story authentically?

Some people move into their stories awkwardly. They change their voice to a storytelling voice (e.g., "Once upon a time"), making them sound fake. Or they just dive into the story without giving any context, resulting in their buyer wondering, "Why the heck are they telling this story?"

Don't make these mistakes. Instead, use one brief statement that explains why you're telling the story, where you could:

1. Acknowledge what the buyer just said.

2. Tell them that this reminds you of a similar situation.

3. Ask if they'd like to learn about it.

Let me give you a few examples:

Story trigger	Story type	Sample *transition in*
Buyer tells you about a problem they have	Industry story	"That's a tough problem indeed. Look, we've been chatting to dozens of companies that are very similar to yours. Would it be helpful if I shared what's impacting them?" → Go into story

Story trigger	Story type	Sample *transition in*
Buyer asks you to share how you can help	Success story	"Sure. Let me give you an example of how we helped another client who was going through similar struggles, OK?" → Go into story
You want to communicate what's unique about you	Differentiation story	"Should I give you an example that gives you a good idea about our approach?" → Go into story
Buyer pushes back	Resistance story	"I understand that price could be an issue. Would it be helpful if I shared an example of a customer who had a similar concern?" → Go into story

That's it. A brief statement that explains why you're sharing the story.

Maybe you noticed in these examples that I didn't use the word "story." Why not? Because some people can have a strong reaction to that word.

They may fear that you're about to waste their time with a 15-minute fairy tale. Or they may put their resistance up because they think that you want to trick them with some *dirty manipulation* tactic.

147

To avoid any negative reaction, replace the word "story" with "example," "case," or "experience."

Step 2: Share the story

Now, we're ready to go into the actual story.

You can share the story you've prepared in one go or pause once or twice to check in with the buyer.

For instance, after you share the challenge, check in with your buyer: "Does that sound familiar in any way?" or "How does that resonate with you?"

Or before proceeding to the response, ask them, "Would it be helpful if I shared what they did to overcome that problem?"

By asking these questions, it will feel more like a conversation and less like a performance. It will also take the pressure off you from having to talk for 2 minutes straight.

Just be mindful that if you check in too many times, it could hurt the flow of the story and could signal that you feel insecure about sharing the story.

But give it a try. See what style works best for you. Maybe for you, it works well to tell the story in one go. Or maybe asking one or two questions throughout your story works better for you. Experiment.

Step 3: Transition out

Imagine sharing a 2-minute story with your buyer. It's a well-crafted story that makes your buyer listen to every word you say. You finish your last sentence and they love it. Now, you say something like, "Ah well, that's my story. What do you think?"

That's a bit awkward, right? Why? Because it puts too much contrast between your story and your normal style of communication. It makes your story appear like a performance and puts the buyer in an uncomfortable situation.

So, what can you say to transition out more smoothly?

1. Recap what you learned from that experience.

2. Ask your buyer about their experience or how they feel about your solution.

To give you a few real-life examples, here are the last sentences of the stories you've read in the previous chapters:

Story type	Sample recap	Question
Connection story	"I realized that you can change someone's day with just a tiny gesture."	"Has that ever happened to you? Was someone very nice to you for no real reason?"
Industry story	"Pharmacies don't find the time to train the staff, offer the services, and put the right billing in place."	"How far are any of these preventing you from offering clinical services?"
Success story	"That's one example of a client using social media as a powerful sales tool."	"Do you feel that a similar approach could work for you?"

Story type	Sample recap	Question
Differentiation story	"When you work with me, I'll be very honest with you."	"Do you feel this approach would work for you?"
Resistance story	"We can help you get access to the technology even if you can't afford it today."	"How do you feel about such an arrangement?"

That's it. One or two sentences that help you transition out of your story and move the focus back to the listener.

Exercise

Pick a story you'd like to share in an upcoming meeting. Then go ahead and think about:

1. How you could transition into the story.

2. Where you could pause to check in with your buyer.

3. How you could transition out of your story.

Even though you don't know exactly what the buyer will say, it's good to think about your options beforehand. This way, it will be easier to move into your story.

Summary

◇ StorySelling is a dialogue, not a monologue

◇ The best storytellers weave the story into their conversations as smoothly as possible

◇ You can do this by explaining why you're sharing the story (transition in), sharing parts of the story, asking the buyer whether they'd like to hear more (share the full story), then asking if the solution could work for them (transition out)

Bringing it together

So far, we've looked at each of the steps separately. Let's look at a sample conversation to see how all the pieces come together:

Person	Sample conversation	Notes
Seller	"So, what's going on with… that is frustrating you or that's problematic from your point of view?"	Asks questions to uncover pain points
Buyer	"Look, the past month our entire IT infrastructure broke down three times…"	Shares pain points
Seller	"Hmm… tough one. You mentioned that the incident could have *pretty bad* consequences. Can you tell me more about that?"	Asks clarifying questions
Buyer	"Sure. By bad consequences, I mean…"	Shares more detail
Seller	"What I hear from you is that the funding could be frozen and your project terminated. Is that correct?"	Paraphrases what has been said
Buyer	"You got it."	Confirms

Person	Sample conversation	Notes
Seller	"That must be really stressful. It reminds me of a situation where one of our customers went through a similar struggle. Would it be helpful if I shared that situation?"	Transitions into story and checks whether the buyer would like to hear it
Buyer	"Sure!"	Confirms
Seller	"4 years back, the CEO of a telco company reached out to us…"	Starts story, giving context
	"Similar to you, their entire IT infrastructure broke down for 5 full days…"	Shares challenge
	"Sounds a bit familiar, right?"	Asks how the challenge resonates
Buyer	"Well. Different industry, but yeah, similar problem."	Confirms
Seller	"Would it be helpful if I shared what they did to overcome that problem?"	Asks whether the buyer would like to hear the remainder of the story
Buyer	"Yes. That'd be great!"	Confirms

Person	Sample conversation	Notes
Seller	"Over 4 weeks, we replaced every single server in the company with new servers that..."	Shares response
	"It's been 3 years now and they haven't had a single incident..."	Shares result
	"Do you feel that something like this could work for you?"	Asks whether the solution could work for buyer
Buyer	"Hmm... could work..."	Responds

Yay, you've made it quite far into the book already.

Great job.

I'm excited for you to start using stories in your upcoming client conversations.

If you've found this book helpful so far, would you do me a small favor and leave an honest review on Amazon? It'll only take a minute, and it would mean the world to me. Plus, it'll help other people like you become amazing storytellers too.

Thanks for spreading the love! You rock!

PART 5

TAKE
ACTION

Beginner storytellers may have a short burst of motivation but then fail to do the work to transform their storytelling skills.

Expert storytellers take consistent action to hone their storytelling skills.

In Part 5, you'll learn how to set your storytelling goals and define and execute an action plan to reach these goals.

Chapter 17

SET YOUR GOALS

"The greatest danger for most of us is not that our aim is too high and we miss it, but that it is too low and we reach it."

— Michelangelo

The fact that you've read so far means you're truly committed to honing your StorySelling skills. Well done for making it a priority.

My objective is to help you truly transform your storytelling skills. I want you to feel excited to share stories in any client conversation. I want others to hang on every word you say. I want you to build more meaningful relationships by sharing stories in all of your interactions.

For you to sacrifice your precious free time and work on your storytelling skills, the desired outcome has to be appealing. Otherwise, it will be very easy to just not work on your storytelling and instead spend time binge-watching Netflix, shopping online, or scrolling through social media.

Let's do 1 minute of silence for all the habits we've broken.

Great! So now, how can we make the outcome appealing?

By defining 2–3 big goals that you'd like to achieve by becoming a better storyteller.

What concrete results would fire you up and make you willing to put in the extra work and effort?

Here are some actual goals from my clients:

- Being promoted to manager by the end of the year
- Speaking at the Sales Enablement Summit in Amsterdam in May
- Joining the President's Club at my company
- Participating in a New York StorySLAM in six months

So, what makes a great goal?

The most common way to set goals is using SMART goals (Specific, Measurable, Achievable, Relevant, and Timely). I like SMART and recommend you use it, but I want to make one adjustment.

Instead of using *achievable* goals, I prefer to use *ambitious* goals.

Why?

Because ambitious goals force you to grow at a quicker pace. You'll need to upgrade your daily habits, skills, and beliefs to reach your ambitious goals.

On the contrary, when setting achievable goals, you'll have less urgency to upgrade your habits, skills, and beliefs. You can basically remain the same person and still achieve a realistic goal.

Let me share my experience.

When I started my business, my goal was to make $50k in a year. This salary seemed like an achievable goal for someone who had just started, and it was enough to cover my expenses.

A few months later, I was in my apartment doing my taxes. After entering all my invoices into the system, I looked at the total sales on the screen. "Shoot. $13k in 6 months. Almost nothing." Panic started to spread: "If I continue like this, I'll be broke in a few months. I'll have to move back to Germany to live with my mum." (No offense, Mum! I love you.)

I shared my worry with my friend Soraya, who recommended the book *The 10X Rule* by Grant Cardone.[13]

One of the principles of the book is to set yourself 10X goals—goals that are 10 times greater than your normal goals.

After reading the book, I thought about my goals and realized that they were not ambitious enough, so I revised them. My new goal was to make $500k in revenue by the end of the year. Much more ambitious than the goal before. Did it feel completely unrealistic at first? Absolutely.

But by repeating my goal and visualizing it every day, it started to feel more attainable. With each day, I became more convinced that it would actually come true. I also started making different decisions. Instead of trying to do everything myself ($50k mindset), I started to outsource more of my work to make the best use of my time ($500k mindset).

A year later, I looked at my earnings reports. I had made $210k. Sure, less than $500k but much more than the $50k that I had originally gone for.

I was super proud to have made that much in my first year since starting my business.

So, with that in mind...

Set yourself ambitious goals. Goals that are much greater than your normal goals. Goals that are big enough to inspire you and hold your attention.

For instance, if your goal was to reach a 100% bonus this year, why not aim for 500%? Or if your plan was to be promoted in 3 years, why not aim to be promoted this year?

Exercise

Take a few minutes and ask yourself: "What is my one big goal that I'd like to reach by becoming a better storyteller?" Pick a goal that fires you up. Something that makes it worthwhile to put in the extra effort.

◇ Summary ◇

⬥ For you to work on your storytelling skills and to sacrifice your precious free time, you have to make the desired outcome enticing

⬥ To do so, you can set yourself 1–2 goals that you'd like to accomplish through the help of storytelling

⬥ Use SMART to set your goals but replace achievable with ambitious

Chapter 18

DEFINE AN ACTION PLAN

"A goal without a plan is just a wish."

– Antoine de Saint-Exupéry,
writer and pioneering aviator

Defining your goals should fire you up to improve your storytelling skills. But knowing your goals is, unfortunately, not enough. If knowing your goals were enough, everybody would be jacked, happy, and rich. As we know, that's not the case.

For you to reach your ambitious goals, you need to define specific actions that will take you there. You need to define the *how*.

What are the actions you need to take to achieve your ambitious goals?

Here are some sample actions from my clients:

Craft stories

- Improvise a story using the 4-step story structure
- Structure, enhance, and simplify a story
- Listen to stories from podcasts, assessing the techniques used to enhance a story

Find stories

- Respond to "how are you?" with a connection story
- Interview a coworker or customer to get new story ideas
- Capture the story in your Story Bank

Build confidence

- Rehearse the story
- Identify and replace any self-limiting beliefs
- Visualize the outcome of an upcoming meeting

Deliver stories

- Do your pre-meeting due diligence
- Practice listening to understand with a random person
- Share the story with a client

Looking at the list of sample actions can be a bit overwhelming. I know! So many options!

So, what actions should you start with?

This depends on you. What area is preventing you from telling more stories the most?

Once you know what is preventing you from telling more stories the most, you can focus on addressing the challenge.

For each goal, pick up to five actions and define when you'll have completed these.

Let's look at an example. Imagine your goal was to use storytelling to close the largest deal in the company in the upcoming quarter.

This is what your action plan could look like:

Actions	Due date
Craft three stories (1x success story, 1x differentiation story, and 1x industry story)	Week 2
Rehearse each story 2–3 times	Week 3
Share stories with coworkers to get feedback	Week 4
Visualize closing the largest deal for 7 days	Week 5
Share a story with the customer	Week 6

Each one of the actions is very specific and has a clear date when it's due. This way, it's easy to track your progress.

Once you've defined your action plan, how can you ensure that you follow through?

Let me share three tips to help you stick to your action plan.

1. Define the minimum action

No doubt, there will be days when you'll feel stressed, angry, or unmotivated. That's what we call life. The first thing to do in these moments is eliminate things that *seem to* cause additional friction (such as taking 30 minutes to craft your success story). While I understand this, I'd encourage you not to eliminate the action altogether but reduce the length or intensity of it.

For example: Instead of rehearsing three stories, you could rehearse one story, or instead of crafting a full story, you could write the first two steps of a story structure. For each action, define the minimum action that you will commit to. No exceptions.

2. Reward yourself

While the actions should ideally be kind of enjoyable, I know it's tough to compete with other dopamine-inducing things in life such as Netflix, Instagram, or solving a Rubik's cube (blindfolded if you want an insane hit of dopamine).

So, we have to find ways to reward ourselves. How?

Before the activity: Reflect on how the action helps you achieve your goal. Imagine your goal coming true. Feel the sense of accomplishment at reaching your goal.

After the activity: Feel grateful for having taken the right steps to reach your goals. Say "Thank you! Thanks for having taken consistent action." Tap yourself on the shoulder and be proud of yourself.

3. Conduct an after-action review (AAR)

An AAR is a structured process of reflecting on the actions you've taken and the results you've achieved. Each week, ideally on the same day (such as Sunday), sit down for a few minutes and reflect upon the progress you've made.

In this session, you can review what happened, why it happened, what went well, and what needs improvement.

The AAR can include the following questions:

1. What did you want to accomplish this week?
2. What did you actually accomplish?
3. What did you do right, so you can do more of those behaviors?
4. What did you do wrong, so you can eliminate those behaviors?
5. What will you do differently next week to stay on target?

Why is it so powerful to do this review? Because it will tell you where you are in relation to where you want to be and will help you spot areas that are blocking you from reaching your goals. By reflecting on these questions regularly, you'll be more likely to stick to your action plan and reach the goals you've set for yourself.

Exercise

Define a concrete action plan to reach your goal. What are the five specific actions and due dates that you'll take to reach your goal?

Action plan templates

Are you looking for templates to define your action plan or to set up your AAR? Go to power-of-storytelling.com/kit and download the templates for free.

Summary

◇ If you want to reach your ambitious goal, you need to have a clear plan on how to get there

◇ By defining five specific actions and corresponding due dates, you'll have a concrete plan to reach your ambitious goal

◇ To help you follow through with your action plan, it helps to 1) define the minimum actions, 2) reward yourself before and after taking the action, and 3) conduct an AAR

CONCLUSION

"There is no greater agony than bearing an untold story inside you."

— Maya Angelou,
poet, memoirist, and civil rights activist

Yay. You did it!

I feel incredibly honored that you've chosen my book to help you transform your storytelling skills. By reading the book and completing the exercises, you're positioning yourself among the top sellers who know how to tell great stories.

After reading the book, you:

- Know how to structure any sales stories, following the 4-step story structure
- Can transform any average moment into an unforgettable story, by using surprise, emotions, and visual moments
- Are clear on which stories work best in sales
- Have a bunch of ideas that you can turn into captivating stories
- Know how to practice your stories so they sound natural

- Have started rewriting the stories you tell yourself
- Are committed to becoming a great listener
- Have a plan that helps you truly transform your skills

Here's one final tip:

Don't wait for your stories to be perfect.

When I started on my journey, I always felt that my stories needed to be perfect. By thinking this way, I put immense pressure on myself and barely told any stories. Without telling any stories, it took me much longer to see any results.

What a missed opportunity. Don't make the same mistake I did. Go out and get your hands dirty. Tell stories in front of your family, friends, or coworkers. Any occasion is a great opportunity to hone your storytelling skills.

Sure, no doubt, there are a few things that you can still work on. But trust me, your stories are already in incredible shape. Give it a go and experience the magic. You have everything it takes to inspire your listeners.

From the bottom of my heart, thank you for embarking on this exciting journey.

P. Humm

Philipp

PS: If you've found this book helpful, would you do me a small favor and leave an honest review on Amazon? It'll only take a minute, and it would mean the world to me. Plus, it'll help other people like you become amazing storytellers too.

Join the free masterclass:

The 3-step formula to build instant trust through storytelling

Learn the proven approach to spot, craft, and deliver the perfect connection story.

By the end of the masterclass, you'll have a few stories you can start using today to build more trusting relationships and win more customers.

Go to power-of-storytelling.com/kit and check out the masterclass for free!

Oh, and you'll get a sneak peek of the book's creator (aka me) and a taste of how cool (or intense) my workshops can be.

Join the StorySelling Facebook community

You are warmly invited to join us in the StorySelling Facebook Group. It's an awesome community of sales experts, entrepreneurs, and consultants who are committed to master the art of storytelling. You'll find tons of useful tips and tricks, real-life sample stories, and regular interviews with experts.

It's a very active group that will support you on your storytelling journey!

Join now: https://www.facebook.com/groups/storysellingtribe

Join the StorySelling program

From reading this book, you have all the tools and techniques you need to become a mesmerizing storyteller. But we often need an additional support system. If you'd like to practice your stories in front of a peer group, get personalized feedback, and be held accountable, check out my StorySelling programs.

Every few months, we work with a small group of ambitious sales professionals to bring their storytelling skills to the next level. You can find our upcoming programs on www.power-of-storytelling.com.

Host a customized program at your company

If you feel that your team's storytelling could be taken up a notch and you don't mind me pushing your team (gently) out of their comfort zones, get in touch with me at info@power-of-storytelling.com. I'd be delighted to support your team through keynotes, workshops, or customized programs.

Stay in touch

Send me a connection request, say hi, or ask me a question. I'd be honored to have you in my network and make sure to get back to you.

You can me find on:

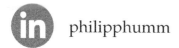 philipphumm

 the_powerofstorytelling

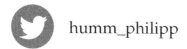 humm_philipp

 philipp-humm

ACKNOWLEDGMENTS

Writing a book is a wild ride—fun, but also super daunting. Impossible to accomplish alone.

I want to thank all the incredible people who have helped me put the pieces of The StorySelling Method together.

First and foremost, I want to thank my family, who have been my rock throughout this whole thing. Your love, loyalty, and support have been my foundation, and I couldn't have done it without you.

To my friends Damian, Brenda, Julia, Mayur, Gina, Victor, Diego, Toola, Jan, Spencer, Enrique, Max, Marius, Jacob, and Steffi—y'all are the real MVPs. You read the book when it was still all over the place, and your encouragement, feedback, and willingness to bounce ideas have helped me massively.

To my business partner, Monica Evason, thanks for keeping me honest and pushing me to be a better person.

To my editors, Ameesha Green and Amanda Lewis, big ups to you both! Your guidance, feedback, and editing have been incredibly helpful.

To the 71 sales experts and frontline sellers who contributed their time, wisdom, and stories to this project. You've made this book what it is today, and I'm honored to have worked with you all.

And finally, to my readers—YOU! Thank you for being here, investing your time, and for engaging with the ideas and insights I've put out there. It's an honor and a privilege to share this journey with you, and I'm grateful for your support and encouragement.

Thank you all!

REFERENCES

1 Chip and Dan Heath, *Made to Stick*

2 https://significantobjects.com/

3 https://greatergood.berkeley.edu/article/item/how_
   stories_change_brain

4 Gerald Zaltman: How Customers Think: Essential Insights
   into the Mind of the Market

5 https://www.nature.com/articles/s41467-020-17255-9

6 Flesch-Kincaid

7 Andy Paul, *Sell without Selling Out* (Kindle 2022,
   Chapter 7)

8 LinkedIn State of Sales Report 2022 United States & Canada
   Edition)

9 https://www.gong.io/blog/talk-to-listen-conversion-
   ratio/

10 https://markmanson.net/vulnerability-in-relationships

11 Matthew Dicks, Storyworthy (Paperback, 2018)

12 https://www.teamusa.org/News/2020/September/26/
   A-Broken-Foot-A-Lost-Friend-Laura-Wilkinson-Looks-
   Back-On-Winning-Gold-At-The-2000-Olympic-Games

13 Grant Cardone, The 10X Rule: The Only Difference
   Between Success and Failure

INTERVIEWEES QUOTED IN THIS BOOK

Name	Role	Page
Luke Floyd	Senior Account Executive at Deel	18
Mark Hunter	Author of *High-Profit Prospecting*	22
Steve Clayton	VP at Microsoft	26
Colleen Stanley	Author of *Emotional Intelligence for Sales Success*	30
Andrew Sykes	CEO of Habits at Work	35
Patricia Fripp	President at Fripp & Associates	41
Niraj Kapur	Author of *Everybody Works in Sales*	45
Evan Kelsay	Senior Director at Seismic Software	49
Dorina Rigo	CEO and Founder of Fit Boots	60
Max Kurth	Sales Manager at Amazon	61
Anthony Iannarino	Author of *Elite Sales Strategies*	67

Name	Role	Page
Scott Von Deylen	VP at Tabula Rasa Healthcare	68
Chantal Humm	Account Executive at Google	69
Larry Kendall	Author of *Ninja Selling*	71
Julia Winkler	Account Manager at Tricycle Europe	74
Victor Ruiz Lafita	Sales Lead at Bigblue	75
Craig Wortmann	Founder of the Kellogg Sales Institute	79
Mike Weinberg	Author of *New Sales. Simplified.*	81 & 145
Brad Harmon	Sales Executive at Oracle	87
Mike Dutter	VP of Sales at Oracle	88
Lee B. Salz	Author of *Sell Different!*	105
Scott Ingram	Account Director at Relationship One	139

WHO'S THIS PHILIPP GUY ANYWAY?

Philipp Humm's mission is to bring out the storyteller that is within each of us.

He has helped thousands of sellers, leaders, and entrepreneurs use stories to inspire in business and beyond. He has worked with some of the leading organizations across the world, including Google, Visa, Oracle, Noom, E.ON, and many more.

Before his storytelling career took off, Philipp worked for nearly a decade in various roles at Uber, Bain & Company, and Blackstone. He discovered his love for performance arts (acting, improv, and storytelling) during his time in New York while completing his MBA at Columbia University. His TEDx talk, "The Secret to Building Confidence," was selected as an Editor's Pick by the global TED organization.

In his free time, Philipp shares stories at open mic nights in Amsterdam, moves his hips at regular bachata parties, and plays Spikeball with friends.

Printed in Great Britain
by Amazon

39016029R00106